Moving to InDesign

David Blatner
Christopher Smith
Steve Werner

PEACHPIT PRESS

❧

David: To Richard

Steve: To Amma and Harry

Christopher: To Grant and Elizabeth

❀

MOVING TO INDESIGN
David Blatner, Christopher Smith, and Steve Werner

Copyright © 2005 by David Blatner, Christopher Smith, and Steve Werner

PEACHPIT PRESS
1249 Eighth Street
Berkeley, California 94710
(800) 283-9444
(510) 524-2178
(510) 524-2221 (fax)

Find us on the World Wide Web at: http://www.peachpit.com
Peachpit Press is a division of Pearson Education

Editor: Nancy Davis
Production coordinator: Lisa Brazieal
Indexer: Caroline Parks
Cover design: Mimi Heft
Cover illustration: Diane Fenster
Interior design and production: David Blatner (moo.com) and Jeff Tolbert

ISBN 0-321-29411-4   686.2
9 8 7 6 5 4 3 2 1   BLa
                            3.05

Printed and bound in the United States of America

overview

contents

Part 3: Building Pages

Part 4: Building Documents

Part 5: Typography

Part 6: Styles

Part 7: Graphics

Part 8: Where Text Meets Graphics

Part 9: Color and Transparency

Appendixes

introduction

Have you ever bought a new cell phone—or a washing machine, or a power tool—and muddled through the instruction manual? The people who write the manual assume that we've never had a cell phone before—or a washing machine or a power tool—so they start from the beginning. Don't forget to plug it in, they remind us, as though we thought electricity comes from the air.

Granted, there is a place for instruction manuals that start from the very beginning (a very good place to start, as Julie Andrews would tell us), but what we often need is a manual that knows what we already understand and just tells us what's different and what's the same. That's what this book is all about. We know you already know how to use QuarkXPress or PageMaker. We know many of you recently added a new tool—Adobe InDesign—to your existing toolbox of desktop publishing applications. We know you want to get up and running as fast as possible. Others of you may be reading this book because you're considering whether you should even start using InDesign.

We've been there; we feel your pain.

Learning a new program is no fun, especially when you're facing a publication deadline. We want to help you learn InDesign faster and easier by leveraging your knowledge, using what you know about QuarkXPress or PageMaker as a springboard to greater efficiency with this new program.

How to Read This Book

Because each chapter of this book covers a basic task or concept—text wrap, for instance, or exporting PDF files—we don't expect many of you will read the whole thing cover to cover. Rather, we think it makes sense to read the first few chapters, just to get up and running, and then skip around the book, gathering what you need when you need it.

Note that we have no intention of having this book cover everything you ever wanted to know about InDesign. Sure, we cover a lot of ground, and we take an in-depth look at many of the features (especially those that have no equivalent in XPress or PageMaker). But we expect that you'll use this book in conjunction with other resources on InDesign (see "For More Information," below).

Why Use InDesign

Before we go any further, we should probably ask an important question: If you already know how to use QuarkXPress or PageMaker, why bother with Adobe InDesign? If you're sitting on the fence about switching, you've probably spent a lot of time asking yourself this recently. If you've already fallen head over heels for InDesign, then your boss, your printer, and your clients are likely asking you. So, let's look at some of the reasons we find InDesign so compelling.

Features

While InDesign, XPress, and PageMaker all have a core set of features which are similar (and sometimes identical), they each have some features that the other does not. For example, QuarkXPress has drag-and-drop text and the ability to export Web-ready HTML, including rollovers and cascading menus—InDesign does none of these things. Nevertheless, if you analyze these programs's feature lists, InDesign is ultimately the overwhelming winner. Here are a few reasons why.

- **User Interface.** InDesign has been life-changing for us because we can start trusting what we see on screen so much more than with XPress or PageMaker. InDesign incorporates a type of "Display PostScript," so you can see what text, bitmapped images, and vector graphics really look like before you print a proof. Plus, there's a Preview mode that hides all guides and non-printing items, an Overprint Preview mode that simulates overprinting inks on screen, and the ability to zoom in to 4,000 percent.

Unlike XPress or PageMaker, you can place guides precisely, lock them, color them, copy-and-paste them, and even put them on a layer. You can turn on a graph-paper document grid for quick alignment. You can truly lock an object (XPress's Lock feature is lame, letting you move and even delete locked objects). You can display your document in more than one window (for multiple views). The list goes on and on.

- **Typographic Features.** If you care about type, InDesign is the program for you. InDesign makes hyphenation and justification decisions based on the look of a whole paragraph rather than one line at a time. Plus, support for hanging punctuation, automatic kerning based on the shape of the characters, and all the OpenType features (like automatic fractions and swashes) means you can get high-quality typography without having to painstakingly do it manually.

- **Graphics and Transparency.** Most folks do their really cool layout work in Photoshop. InDesign's transparency features mean that you can spend more time doing *layout* in your page-layout application. For example, because InDesign understands native Photoshop (.PSD) files and retains their transparency, you may never have to make a clipping path in Photoshop again; just erase the background to the checkerboard transparency and import into InDesign. Similarly, you don't have to use an XTension or switch to Photoshop just to make a drop shadow or to feather the edges of an object because InDesign has these features built in. To all you cynics out there: Yes, this stuff really does print beautifully; it doesn't crash RIPs or cause service bureaus to spontaneously combust (we show you how in the Printing section of the book).

- **Tables.** InDesign's table features far outshine XPress's or PageMaker's, letting you set automatic alternating fills or strokes, link tables across pages, and even convert Microsoft Word and Excel tables into editable InDesign tables.

- **Printing and Exporting.** A number of output providers (who have notoriously long memories) were burned by the poor printing architecture in InDesign 1.0 and 1.5. But Adobe made huge advances in version 2, and now many service providers prefer InDesign CS over XPress or PageMaker! It now features built-in preflighting, the ability to export high-quality PDF files directly to disk (without Distiller), embedding fonts in EPS files, and generating DSC-compliant device-independent PostScript (something we techno-geeks have been asking from Quark for 12 years).

- **Other Stuff.** The list of features InDesign has and XPress or PageMaker do not goes on and on: It's scriptable on Windows as well as the Macintosh. You can edit all the keyboard shortcuts. If you crash (all software crashes sooner or later), InDesign recovers your document so you don't lose much (if any) work. You can base master pages on other master pages or turn a document page into a master page. It is Unicode compliant, so you can set multiple languages (even those with non-Roman character sets) in the same document. And more!

Granted, features aren't everything. But features are like tools on a Swiss Army knife—the right feature at the right time can be a major lifesaver! Of course, there was no one feature that convinced us that InDesign is a great tool; rather it is the broad assortment of InDesign's features that make our work easier.

On the other hand, if you absolutely cannot live without one of the features that is only found in XPress or PageMaker, then you're stuck (until Adobe adds that feature).

Performance

One of the better reasons to stick with XPress 4 or 5 or PageMaker 7 has been those programs's performance on older, slower computers. InDesign's feature set comes at a cost: It's RAM and processor hungry—anything less than a Pentium 4 or G4 processor with 256 MB of RAM will make your InDesign experience frustrating, especially with longer documents. Generally, any machine on which you'd be happy running Photoshop will also support InDesign. (QuarkXPress 6 requires a fast processor and lots of RAM, too.)

But computing power is only half the equation when it comes to being productive in a program. In 2002 (and again in 2004), Pfeiffer Consulting conducted extensive tests exploring what happened to business productivity when companies began to use InDesign. The results were fascinating (you can read them yourself at *www.pfeifferreport.com*). In short, they found that what saved the most time was not the raw speed of the computer or the software, but was reducing the number of steps required to build a document.

At first, it made us crazy that InDesign imports Microsoft Word documents significantly slower than XPress or PageMaker (particularly long documents). Then we found that while we lose a little time at import, we gain a lot more time because InDesign does so much automatically (or with a single step) that we had to do manually in XPress or PageMaker (with many steps). For example, anyone who has spent the afternoon trying to get text to look just right by adding manual line breaks, discretionary hyphens, and other typographic tweaks will be astonished at how little of that is necessary because of InDesign's paragraph composer. (That said, Adobe engineers have assured us that they're working on making the import feature faster in future versions of InDesign.)

Similarly, InDesign saves steps by letting you make drop shadows in the page-layout program, drawing a frame for you when you import text or graphics (if you don't already have one), converting Word and Excel tables to editable tables upon import, and even maintaining the editability of copy-and-pasted vector artwork from Illustrator or FreeHand.

The Pfeiffer Report found astonishing efficiency increases in some areas of work (like making PDF files) and found that InDesign equalled XPress in other areas. In their benchmark testing, it took designers two to three times longer to create a document in XPress than in InDesign.

What's Your ROI?

For many people, especially at larger companies, the biggest hurdle to using InDesign is not learning the features (you've already got that handled by buying this book) but convincing "the suits." After all, arguments like "It's got more features!" and "I can go home early if I use it" don't go over well with those folks we affectionately call the bean counters.

When approaching your boss, you need to use phrases like "return on investment" (ROI) and "increasing workflow integration for gigahertz productivity enhancements." (The latter expression doesn't actually mean anything, but it's very impressive.)

Of course, measuring ROI in the publishing industry is difficult. For a small design firm, the investment is simply the cost of the new software and a couple of books or training classes to help you learn it. The return can be anything from cooler designs that help you get more clients to saving time on producing a big job.

Larger companies tend to think about the cost of retraining (both in money and hours lost from the production cycle), and the returns come in reducing headcount and expenses. Fortunately, the Pfeiffer Report also looked at ROI issues, briefly mentioning how Australia's largest magazine publisher, ACP, cut their prepress costs in *half* while moving 40 magazines (including *Cosmopolitan* and 7 weeklies) to InDesign. Designers and the production team put one issue of a magazine to bed with QuarkXPress and the next issue was created—cover to cover—with InDesign. It was a highly successful operation, and the company reportedly saved so much money (in the relative cost of the software plus in reducing prepress expenses) that they could afford to buy new computers for everyone (we're still waiting for ours).

Add a Tool, Don't Replace It

Our publisher keeps calling this a "switcher book," for people who want to switch to InDesign. Our response is: No, it's for people who want to *add* InDesign to their repertoire. We expect that there are very few people who will be in the position to completely drop QuarkXPress or PageMaker, even though we have no intention of creating any new documents with those programs. Therefore, for the foreseeable future, it's likely that you'll need to know how to use two layout programs (or at least keep someone on staff who does).

But doesn't InDesign open XPress and PageMaker documents? Sure it does, but not necessarily perfectly. In Appendixes A and B, we explain what does and doesn't translate and how you should best use this feature.

Our colleague Sandee Cohen notes that people who start using InDesign often try to fit it into the same workflow they're accustomed to. Sure, you can replace XPress with InDesign and keep doing everything else the same, but you're going to miss out on a lot InDesign has to offer. Using InDesign is all about finding new and better ways of working—integrating all your tools together for maximum efficiency.

For More Information

As we said earlier, as deep as we can go in the next 400 pages, we don't expect to answer every question you ever have about InDesign. For example, we don't cover how to script InDesign or import/export XML. Fortunately, there are other resources out there. Here's a few places you can go for more information.

- *Real World Adobe InDesign CS.* While we are a bit biased (this book was written by David Blatner and long-time industry expert Olav Martin Kvern), this is also the book recommended by members of the InDesign development team at Adobe.

- *Adobe InDesign CS Visual QuickStart Guide.* Sandee Cohen offers a wonderful step-by-step introduction to InDesign. We tend to like this better than the *Adobe InDesign Classroom in a Book*, though that one is good, too.

- **Adobe InDesign Web Site.** Most corporate Web sites are filled with marketing materials. You'll find plenty of that at Adobe, but it's alongside excellent useful information, too. It's definitely worth a trip to *www.adobe.com/products/indesign*. Also, the answers to many of your most puzzling InDesign questions can be answered by the knowledgeable and helpful volunteers in the InDesign User to User Forums at *www.adobe.com/support/forums/main.html*

- **InDesign Magazine.** Creativepro.com, in conjunction with our own David Blatner, launched *InDesign Magazine* in July, 2004. The PDF-based magazine is packed with in-depth features, reviews, and tutorials. You can find more information at *www.indesignmag.com*

- **InDesign Users Groups.** At the time of this writing, there are InDesign Users Groups in San Francisco, Seattle, Chicago, Atlanta, Portland, Reno, Minneapolis, Milwaukee, Boston, Washington, DC, New York City, and Melbourne, Australia; we expect more to appear soon (see *www.indesignusergroup.com*). If you've got one near you, check it out.

Acknowledgements

We'd like to give special thanks to a few of the people who helped us turn a crazy idea into the book you're now holding. First, many thanks to the folks at Adobe who gave us a great product and have helped support this book, including Will Eisley, Michael Wallen, Tim Cole, Mark Neimann-Ross, Thomas Phinney, Lonn Lorenz, and Olav Martin "Ole" Kvern.

Thanks to our Peachpit editors, Nancy Davis and Serena Herr, for their extraordinary patience and (usually) gentle nudges to get it done. To Lisa Brazieal for her help in riding this wild Ducati all the way to the printer. To Conrad Chavez, for his excellent technical editing and to Jeff Tolbert for his great (and fast) production on the first edition. And to Caroline Parks, whose eagle eye produced a terrific index.

Our sincere appreciation for a wealth of good information goes to Sandee "Vector Babe" Cohen, Deke "The Man" McClelland, Scott Citron, the InDesign beta testers, and participants in the BlueWorld InDesign list and the InDesign User to User Forums.

Steve: "Thanks to Bent Kjolby and the staff at Rapid Lasergraphics for giving me the freedom to develop and teach my classes. Thanks to my students, who have taught me so much. Thanks to Astrid Wasserman of MediaLive and Thad McIlroy for encouraging me to teach at Seybold Seminars. And finally thanks to Harry and all our friends who have provided me with the support I needed during the months it took to write this book."

Christopher: "My sincerest gratitude to my own Creative Sweet: Jennifer Smith, author, creative genius, loving mother and perfect wife. Thanks also to extraordinary AGI instructor Greg Heald for generously sharing his PageMaker knowledge. And to my colleagues David and Steve, it is an absolute pleasure working with you both!"

David: "My deepest appreciation goes to my beloved wife, Debbie, and our delightful sons, Gabriel and Daniel, who are such blessings in my life. I couldn't have finished this book without the help of Don and Snookie, as well as a friendly boost from the FlipSide coffeehouse. Thanks, too, to a host of generous friends and family who remind me that as much as I like digital, analog is even better."

PART 1

Top Ten Common Pitfalls

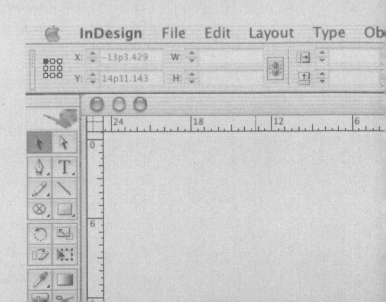

Top Ten "Gotchas" for QuarkXPress Users

We're asked this question all the time: "How long will it take for me to learn InDesign?" The answer, of course, is "It depends." If you're an Adobe Illustrator user, for instance, you'll probably pick up InDesign quickly because so much of InDesign's interface is based on its older sibling. But if you're a hard-core QuarkXPress user without a strong Illustrator background, you should probably prepare yourself for three days of a sore head (from banging it on the nearest wall). That's how long it seems to take for XPress users to get over their XPress bias, figure out how InDesign does it, and come to the conclusion that, wow, Adobe actually did it right.

But in the meantime, we recommend taking the pain reliever of your choice and reading the following ten solutions to the most common "gotchas" you'll encounter.

"Where are the Item and Content tools?"

InDesign replaces QuarkXPress's Item and Content tools with three tools: the Selection tool, the Direct Selection tool, and the Type tool. These three tools offer more control, but they also take much more getting used to. For example, the Selection tool (the black arrow) is almost identical to the Item tool in XPress, but if you double-click with it on a text frame, InDesign automatically switches to the Type tool and places the cursor where you clicked.

The Direct Select tool (the white arrow) acts sort of like the Content tool when it comes to images (you use it to move an image inside a frame), but it also edits the shape of frames, just like in Illustrator. The Type tool not only lets you type and edit text, but you can even use it to drag out a text frame!

"I see the picture box tools, but where are the tools for text boxes?"

While InDesign technically does have text frames, graphic frames, and contentless frames, ultimately the distinctions are somewhat meaningless because any frame can be turned into any other kind of frame at any time. The frame-drawing tools that have an "X" in them in the Tool palette (see Figure 1-1) draw graphic frames (what XPress calls "picture boxes"), but if you click on one of these with the Type tool or use the File>Place command to import text while an empty graphic frame is selected on your page, then InDesign automatically turns it into a text frame on the fly. You can do the same thing with the contentless frames created with the Rectangle, Oval, or Polygon shape tools.

Similarly, you can draw out a text frame with the Type tool. However, if you later click on an empty text frame with the Selection tool and use the Place command to import a graphic, then InDesign changes the frame into a graphic frame and puts the picture in it. We talk more about drawing frames in Chapter 6.

Figure 1-1
Tools for drawing frames

"I can't find text leading!"

Adobe, in all its wisdom, has determined that leading should be a character attribute rather than paragraph formatting, so leading shows up next to the font size field in the Character and Control palettes. This means that you can apply a different leading value to each character of a paragraph—InDesign assigns a leading value for each line of a paragraph based on the largest leading value in the line.

If you find this annoying (QuarkXPress users almost universally do), then turn on the checkbox labelled Apply Leading to Entire Paragraphs in the Text panel of the Preferences dialog box. From then on, you can just place the cursor anywhere within a paragraph, and when you change leading, the whole paragraph is affected.

"Why do I always get the wrong font and size when I start typing?"

Sometimes you'll draw out a text frame with the Type tool and start typing and the font will be completely different than you expect. In XPress, the default text formatting for any text box is based on the Normal font. InDesign, however, has a more complicated (but potentially more powerful) way to handle defaults: Any text formatting you choose while no text frames are selected—font size, leading, color, and so on—becomes the default formatting for that document. If no documents are open, then those attributes become the defaults for all new documents you create.

By the way, this behavior applies to the shape tools, too (the ones that create contentless rectangles, ovals, and polygons). If you pick a fill or stroke color or stroke weight when these tools are selected but no object on the page is, those attributes become the defaults for those tools in this document.

"I can't click on master page items!"

If you put an object on a master page in QuarkXPress and then switch back to a document page, that object is immediately editable. This seems cool until you accidentally mess up your layout by accidentally changing one or more master page items. InDesign is different: It won't even let you select a master page item unless you really intend to.

When you *do* need to select and edit a master page item, try this: Shift-Option-click/Shift-Alt-click on it. That releases it from the master page (it's called *overriding*). Or, you can choose Override All Master Page Items from the Pages palette flyout menu to release all the items on a spread. See Chapter 16 for more information about this.

Note that you do *not* need to override master page items when you're importing text or graphics into your document (see Chapters 19 and 28).

"How am I supposed to link text boxes together without a Link tool?"

In QuarkXPress, you use the Link and Unlink tools in the Tool palette to control text threading. InDesign uses the PageMaker method: Each text

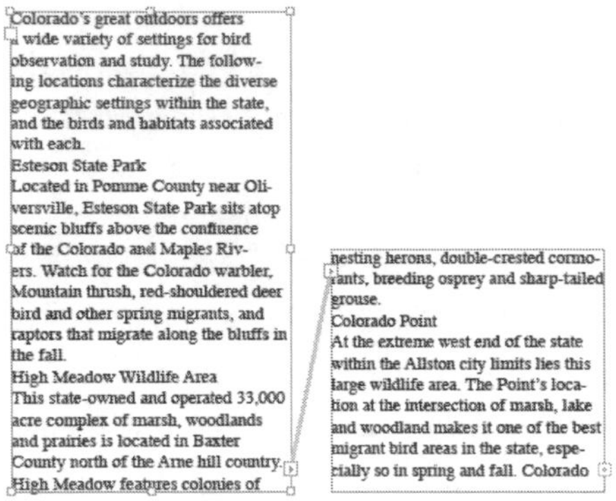

Figure 1-2
In InDesign, the in and out ports (for text threading) are in the upper-left and lower-right corners of text frames.

Colorado's great outdoors offers a wide variety of settings for bird observation and study. The following locations characterize the diverse geographic settings within the state, and the birds and habitats associated with each.
Esteson State Park
Located in Pomune County near Oliversville, Esteson State Park sits atop scenic bluffs above the confluence of the Colorado and Maples Rivers. Watch for the Colorado warbler, Mountain thrush, red-shouldered deer bird and other spring migrants, and raptors that migrate along the bluffs in the fall.
High Meadow Wildlife Area
This state-owned and operated 33,000 acre complex of marsh, woodlands and prairies is located in Baxter County north of the Arne hill country.
High Meadow features colonies of

nesting herons, double-crested cormorants, breeding osprey and sharp-tailed grouse.
Colorado Point
At the extreme west end of the state within the Allston city limits lies this large wildlife area. The Point's location at the intersection of marsh, lake and woodland makes it one of the best migrant bird areas in the state, especially so in spring and fall. Colorado

frame has an in port and an out port that you can see when you select the frame with the Selection or Direct Select tool (see Figure 1-2). To link two frames together, click on one of the ports with one of the selection tools, and then click anywhere on top of another frame. (If you click on the in port first, you're linking *to* this frame; if you click on the out port first, you're linking *from* this frame to another one.) We cover text threading in more detail in Chapter 20.

"Why does creating or editing a color or style affect objects on my page?"

When you create a color using either the Color or the Swatches palette (see Chapter 38 for the difference), InDesign automatically applies the color to any objects selected on your page. Similarly, if you double-click on a name in the Swatches palette, Paragraph Styles, or Character Styles palette (to edit the color or style), the color or style is applied to anything you have selected. This can be crazy-making if you don't expect it. There are several workarounds.

First, get in the habit of pressing Command-Shift-A/Ctrl-Shift-A (or choosing Edit>Deselect All) before you edit or create anything. Second, you can right-button click (or Control-click on the Macintosh) on a paragraph or character style to edit it without applying it. Or you can hold down Command-Option-Shift/Ctlr-Alt-Shift when you double-click on a style or color name to edit it without applying it.

"How do I resize, color, or adjust pictures?"

It's really important to pay attention to what is selected on your page and with what tool you've selected it. If you select a picture with the Selection tool, InDesign chooses the frame and the picture inside it. If you resize now (with the Scale tool, the Control or Transform palette scale fields, or by

Command-Shift-dragging/Ctrl-Shift-dragging) you'll rescale the frame and the picture. Notice that the Control or Transform palette then shows that the image is scaled at 100%—you need to click on the image with the Direct Select tool to see the true scaling of the picture itself.

If you click on the frame with the Direct Select tool, your changes will affect just the frame. If you click inside the frame (on the picture) with the Direct Select tool, you'll affect the picture but not the frame. To colorize a grayscale TIFF, for example, you need to click on the image with the Direct Select tool. To cut it out and put it in another frame, you also need to use the Direct Select tool; then select Edit>Cut, choose the other frame (with either selection tool) and choose Edit>Paste Inside.

"How do I get rid of my guides?"

In QuarkXPress, you can get rid of a guide by clicking on it and dragging it out of the document window. That won't work in InDesign—the window just scrolls around. Instead, remember that InDesign treats guides just like page objects, so you can delete one by clicking on it and pressing the Delete key. You can even use Edit>Cut to put the guide on the clipboard if you want to paste it on another page.

To delete all the guides on your page or spread, first press Command-Option-G/Ctrl-Alt-G to select all the guides, then press Delete. Alternately, you can select Layout>Create Guides, turn on the Remove Existing Ruler Guides checkbox, and click OK.

"Where is that XPress feature I always use?"

InDesign offers more features than QuarkXPress, but that doesn't mean that it matches every feature XPress has. For example, there's no way to apply a custom halftone screen to an imported image, create a font-wide kerning table, specify hexachrome colors, or export HTML Web pages.

However, in some cases, InDesign does have the same or similar feature, but it's been renamed or the user interface is different. If you can't find a "Collect for Output" feature, try File>Package. Need to set the runaround for an object? Use the Text Wrap palette. Want to turn on Suppress Printout for something? Use the Attributes palette. Looking for a way to draw a starburst? Choose one of the two Polygon tools, then double-click on the tool's icon to set its preferences (including Inset, which turns a polygon into a starburst).

2

Top Ten "Gotchas" for PageMaker Users

If you're an Adobe PageMaker user, you've likely been using it for many years, and the idea of switching to another program—even a different Adobe program—is anathema to you. Nevertheless, you see the writing on the wall, you know that PageMaker is a dead end street, and you're trying to stay upbeat as you tackle this new whippersnapper, InDesign CS. Fortunately, not only do PageMaker and InDesign share many core features, as Adobe products they also share a common user interface.

But the two applications are not identical. InDesign has capabilities that PageMaker users have only dreamed of, and we've found that InDesign allows you to work smarter and faster. This chapter addresses some of the most common "gotchas," or pitfalls, that PageMaker users encounter when moving to InDesign.

"When I move from page to page, things I leave on the pasteboard disappear."

PageMaker's pasteboard is based on a traditional "art board" approach—you can place an object from your page out the pasteboard, then change the page (the art board), and the object out the pasteboard is still there for you to use. InDesign, however, uses the QuarkXPress approach to the pasteboard: There's just one huge pasteboard on which all the page spreads sit. Another way to look at this is that the pasteboard is unique for each spread.

The result is that an object placed on the pasteboard disappears when you switch to a new page.

InDesign, like PageMaker, does have an Entire Pasteboard command (View>Entire Pasteboard) that zooms out to allow you to see the pasteboard's contents, but only the objects placed on that page's pasteboard can be viewed.

As in PageMaker, it's not advisable to leave items on InDesign's pasteboard indefinitely. Instead, use InDesign's Library feature to keep track of objects that you may need to use again (File>New: Library). You can drag and drop text frames, graphic frames, and even entire page layouts in and out of a floating library palette as needed. Because the library palette is a separate InDesign file, you can access it from anywhere in your layout, or even from multiple InDesign documents.

"I can't find the Cropping tool."

PageMaker's Cropping tool is cool because it lets you specify which part of an image should be visible. Unfortunately, InDesign doesn't normally have a Cropping tool. Instead, you have to use two tools: The Selection tool and the Direct Select tool.

After you place an image into a graphic frame in InDesign, you can drag the frame's handles with the Selection tool to crop the image down. In both PageMaker and InDesign, the cropped areas of the image (the parts outside the frame edge) aren't really deleted; they're just hidden by the frame boundaries—like seeing a portion of the image through a window.

To move the image inside that window (frame), you must use the Direct Selection tool. Click and drag on the image itself to move it around inside the graphic frame. If you click and hold the mouse button for more than a second before moving it, you can see the placed image in its entirety, with the masked areas ghosted back (see Figure 2-1).

If switching between these tools to resize and move images and their frames proves too cumbersome, or if you long for the all-in-one functionality of PageMaker's Cropping tool, then Adobe has an answer for you. The Adobe PageMaker Plug-In Pack adds eight popular PageMaker features to the standard InDesign feature set. One of these is the Position tool, which gives you all of the resizing and moving capability of the Selection and Direct Selection tools in one context-sensitive tool. The Position tool simply changes functionality based on whether you rest the cursor over a frame's handles (letting you resize or crop the frame) or the content within it (letting you move the picture in the frame).

Figure 2-1
The Direct Selection tool lets you move an image inside a frame.

If you click and hold for a moment, you can see the cropped portion ghosted back.

"How do I create booklets like I do with Build Booklet in PageMaker?"

A popular feature of PageMaker that is not available in the standard release of Adobe InDesign CS is the Build Booklet plug-in. In PageMaker, this imposition feature let you rearrange pages of a document into printer spreads for printing, folding, trimming, and binding.

Fortunately, the Adobe PageMaker Plug-In Pack includes the InBooklet Special Edition (SE) plug-in (see Figure 2-2). InBooklet includes complete control over margins, gaps, bleed, creep, and crossover traps in the following imposition styles: 2-up saddle stitch, 2-up perfect bound, and 2-, 3-, or 4-up consecutive. You can even preview your page imposition in

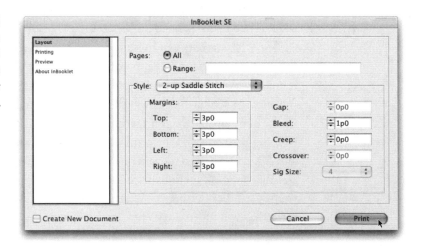

Figure 2-2
ALAP's InBooklet SE comes with the Adobe PageMaker Plug-in Pack.

the InBooklet dialog box to see how your pages will be output using this plug-in. For even more features, check out the full version of InBooklet at *www.alap.com*.

"I always avoided QuarkXPress because it used frames for everything. Now InDesign is the same!"

Actually, PageMaker has also always used frames to hold both text and graphics—it's just that the frames were usually invisible. For example, a "text block" in PageMaker is just a frame, but you can only see its top and bottom edges when you click on it. With that in mind, InDesign's frames are virtually identical to PageMaker's. You can draw a frame and then put content into it, or you can use the File>Place command to import text or graphics without a frame (InDesign creates a frame and inserts the contents for you automatically). InDesign lets you hide the frame's edges (View>Hide Frame Edges) to avoid that cluttered look on your screen.

When it comes to drawing frames or shapes on your page, InDesign's Frame and Shape tools are virtually identical to PageMaker's. The frames themselves do have a few minor cosmetic changes. For example, the In and Out ports used for linking text frames act pretty much the same in the two programs, but in InDesign they're located at the upper-left and lower-right corners (instead of PageMaker's placement at the top and bottom of the frame; see Figure 1-2, in the previous chapter).

"Where's the automatic bullets and numbering that I used in PageMaker?"

The PageMaker Plug-In Pack provides Bulleted List and Numbered List icons (in a PageMaker-style toolbar) for quick and easy formatting. You can choose Bullets and Numbering from the Paragraph palette submenu to specify further formatting options, use the Preview option to view your (unsaved) changes as you work, and easily build automated bullets or numbering into your paragraph styles (see Figure 2-3).

Note that the Adobe PageMaker Plug-In Pack for InDesign also includes a Data Merge plug-in, a Template Browser with professionally-designed templates, and a (previously unavailable) publication converter for PageMaker 6.0 files. Although the Plug-In Pack is an additional cost, many PageMaker users find its features irreplaceable as they make the transition to an InDesign workflow.

Figure 2-3

Bullets and
Numbering Options

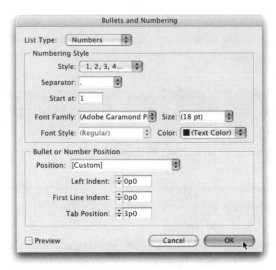

"How do I manage linked images?"

In PageMaker you'd use the Links Manager, Link Options, and Link Info
dialog boxes to manage linked graphics. In InDesign these functions are
all handled by the Links palette (Window>Links; see Figure 2-4). The
palette displays warning icons to notify you when a linked image is missing, has been modified, or is on the pasteboard. Buttons at the bottom of
the palette allow you to easily relink or update the graphic. Choosing Link
Information from the Links palette menu (or double-clicking on the link
in the palette) displays image details like the size, color space, file type,
modification date, and current location of the source graphic.

Figure 2-4

Links palette

One feature missing from InDesign is the ability to simultaneously update multiple links to graphics stored in the same location. InDesign requires you to update each individual link by choosing its specific source location. While this prevents you from inadvertently relinking to the wrong source graphic, it can be more time-consuming.

However, you can use this trick: Once you've updated your first graphic on the Links palette, click in the blank space below the link names to deselect them all. Then when you click the Update button, it will update all the remaining links.

"I miss some of the keyboard shortcuts I used in PageMaker."

Since the user interfaces of PageMaker and InDesign are very similar, you'll find that many commonly-used keyboard shortcuts are the same. Command-D/Ctrl-D, for example, is the shortcut for Place in both applications. For those shortcuts that differ, InDesign allows you to edit your keyboard shortcuts (Edit>Keyboard Shortcuts). In this dialog box, you can choose an existing set of shortcuts (including those for QuarkXPress 4.0), or create your own set and change, create or replace existing shortcuts. (See Chapter 5 for more information.)

And, in case this seems like too much work for a few keyboard shortcuts, the Adobe PageMaker Plug-In Pack again attempts to bridge the gap between programs. It provides PageMaker 7.0-compatible keyboard shortcuts that allow you to continue working with all of your favorites from PageMaker.

"Is there any way to import my PageMaker dictionary and scripts?"

Unfortunately, at this time there is no functionality in InDesign for importing your user dictionaries and/or scripts from PageMaker. When you use the Dictionary feature in InDesign (Edit>Dictionary), it creates hyphenation and spelling lists that are stored, by default, outside the document on the computer where InDesign is installed. You can also store these exception lists inside any InDesign document, which makes it easier when you move that document to other computers. (See Chapter 21 for more on dictionaries.)

PageMaker's scripts have to be rewritten from scratch. The good news is the InDesign is even more scriptable than PageMaker, and you can use AppleScript (on the Mac), VisualBasic (in Windows), or JavaScript (cross-platform).

"I can select items in a stack, but when I try to move a lower item, the top one is selected again."

We've already seen that PageMaker and InDesign share a number of common features. This is no accident, as common features allow for an easier transition from one program to the other. The following technique has been a favorite of PageMaker users for years, and now it's available in InDesign.

To click through (and select) individual stacked items on an InDesign page, simply hold down your Command/Ctrl key while clicking repeatedly on the top item in the stack. With each click, InDesign selects the next item down in the stack. (Be sure, however, to click on an area where the objects are overlapping). You can then move your cursor to drag that lower item to a new location. (Remember not to release the mouse button until you're done moving it). If you do release the mouse button too soon, don't fret: You can still move the object by dragging its centerpoint "handle."

"Where do I set the starting page number for my document?"

In PageMaker, you can set the starting page number for your document by typing a number in the Start page # field in the Document Setup window (when opening a new document, or via File>Document Setup later). This allows for the renumbering of pages, as in the building of sections, as the document was being created.

In InDesign, however, you define your page numbering using the Numbering & Section Options dialog (choose Layout>Numbering & Section Options; see Figure 2-5). This dialog box also offers the added capability of applying unique section prefixes, numbering styles, and section markers. The section page numbering is applied to whatever page is currently selected in the Pages palette.

Figure 2-5
You can set page
numbering for any
section.

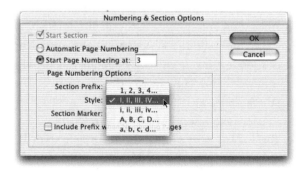

PART 2

The User Interface

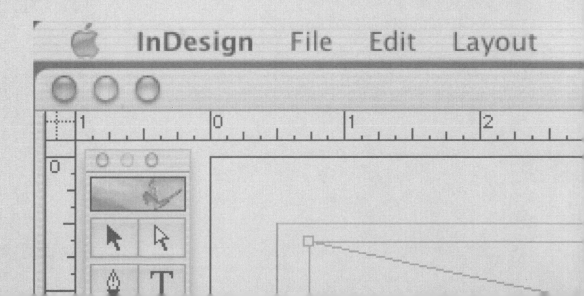

3

The Tools Palette

InDesign's toolbox borrows heavily from other Adobe applications, most notably Adobe Illustrator. Several tools are also identical to those in QuarkXPress.

InDesign's Tools palette can be positioned in the traditional two columns, or in a single vertical column (like XPress's). You can also position it horizontally as a single row (like Microsoft Word's; see Figure 3-1). To change the palette layout, click the maximize window button at the top of the palette (Windows) or double-click the bar at the top of the palette (Macintosh). Or, you can use the General section of InDesign's Preferences dialog box to set the display of the tools palette. If you accidentally close the Tools palette, you can easily re-open the palette by selecting Tools from the Window menu.

Each tool has a key command associated with it (see Figure 3-2). As long as you are not entering or editing text, you can use the key commands to access any of the tools. Use the Tab key to show or hide all palettes. Use Shift-Tab to show or hide all palettes except the Tools palette.

Tools for Selecting and Moving Objects

The Selection tool and Direct Selection tool are both used for selecting objects on your page. The Selection tool (press V) is used to select objects and their contents together. For example, you can use the Selection tool to move a frame and the picture it contains to a new location on a page.

Use the Direct Selection tool (press A) to manipulate the contents of a picture frame. You can also use this tool to select and modify individual

Figure 3-1
Tools palette layouts

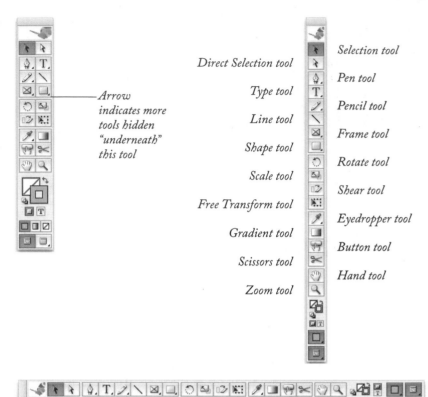

Arrow indicates more tools hidden "underneath" this tool

Direct Selection tool

Type tool

Line tool

Shape tool

Scale tool

Free Transform tool

Gradient tool

Scissors tool

Zoom tool

Selection tool

Pen tool

Pencil tool

Frame tool

Rotate tool

Shear tool

Eyedropper tool

Button tool

Hand tool

points or segments of a frame or path. The appearance of the Direct Select tool changes subtly depending upon the position of the cursor. The direct select arrow displays a small line if a line segment or portion of a frame will be selected or manipulated, while it displays a hollow white dot adjacent to the arrow if an individual point will be selected or modified. A solid dot is displayed adjacent to the cursor's arrow if an entire object is being selected or modified.

See Chapter 7 for more information on selecting objects.

Type Tools

The Type tool (press T) and Path Type tool (press Shift-T) can be used for adding or editing text within frames and on paths, respectively. However, you can also use the Type Tool for creating frames. Click and drag with this tool to quickly build a frame that is ready for you to enter or import text.

Figure 3-2
Keyboard shortcuts
for selecting tools

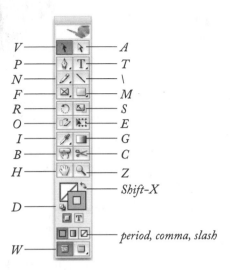

Drawing Tools

Use the drawing tools to build lines or frames. We cover each of these in more detail when we discuss creating and editing shapes in Chapter 8.

Pen

Use the pen tools to create Bézier lines and frames. Use the Pen tool (press P) to draw shapes. Use the closely related Add Anchor Point tool to add points to an existing path or frame, or the Delete Anchor Point tool to remove points from an existing path, while the Convert Direction Point tool modifies the direction of line segments.

Pencil

You can use the Pencil tool (press N) for creating free-form paths, or for building frames—but only if you have a steady hand. Select the Smooth and Erase tools, hidden underneath the Pencil tool, to help create a perfect path. Use these tools if you haven't had the time to master the Pen tools.

Line

To create a straight line, use the Line tool (press the backslash key). Although the Pencil or Pen tools also work, they require a very steady hand or the use of modifier keys (like the Shift key) to keep your lines straight. Hold down the Shift key while dragging with this tool to create straight lines.

Frame

The three Frame tools (press F) allow you to draw rectangular, oval or polygon frames. These frames may contain either text or graphics. You can draw a perfectly square or circular frame by holding down the Shift key when using the oval and rectangle tools. You can also draw a frame from the center of where you have clicked by holding down the Option/ Alt key while drawing the frame.

Set the number of sides in the polygon (or make the polygon into a starburst) by double-clicking on the Polygon tool prior to drawing with it. You can also draw a specific size rectangle or oval frame by clicking once on the page after selecting either of these tools.

Shape

The Shape tools work identically to the Frame tools, however the frames created by the Shape tools have a default stroke (border) around them. While they are intended to serve as graphical elements and not frames, shapes and frames are really interchangeable—you can place text or graphics inside of objects created with either the Shape or Frame tools.

Editing Tools

As we mentioned earlier, it is important to note whether you have selected the frame or the contents of the frame, because the following editing tools modify whatever is selected, so be certain you have mastered the selection tools before venturing into the editing tools.

Rotate

Select the object you wish to rotate then drag with this tool to change the rotation. Where you click with this tool also sets the axis of rotation. To rotate around a specific point, use the Control palette instead.

Scale

Use the Scale tool (press S) to increase or decrease the size of a selected object on the page, including text and picture frames.

Shear

With the Shear tool (press O) you can take an object on your page and apply a skew that'll make your eyes twitch. You can easily over-manipulate objects with this tool, so take advantage of InDesign's multiple undo feature if you find your objects in an awkward position.

Free Transform

You can use the Free Transform tool (press E) to rotate and scale objects. To scale, select one or more objects, choose this tool, and drag one of the corner or side handles in the direction you wish to scale. To rotate, click outside the bounding box and drag. Unlike the Shear tool, which can move in multiple directions concurrently, this tool requires separate actions to rotate or to scale.

Eyedropper

You can use the Eyedropper tool (press I) to copy colors or text formatting from one location to another without building a swatch, or a paragraph or character style. Double click on the Eyedropper tool to set preferences relating to what it will duplicate when copying text formatting.

To copy the color from an imported image, move the Eyedropper tool (the icon should appear "filled" with white) over the image and click once (now the icon should change to be "filled" with black). The color your clicked on should fill the eyedropper and should also be shown in the Color palette and either the fill or stroke color in the bottom of the Tools palette—depending on which is currently active. You can then apply the color to any InDesign object or save it as a swatch.

If you have already selected a color and would like to replace it with another color, hold down the Option/Alt key while clicking with the Eyedropper tool and the tool becomes white and points down and to the left, indicating that it is ready to pick up another color if you click.

The Eyedropper tool definitely takes some getting used to; we cover it more fully in Chapter 38.

Measure

You can use the Measure tool (press K), which is tucked under the Eyedropper tool, to identify the exact size and location of objects on your page. Click and drag with this tool around the area you wish to measure and measurements are displayed in the Info palette.

Gradient

You can use the Gradient tool (press G) to modify the length and direction of existing gradients or to apply a gradient to one or more selected objects. One or more objects must first be selected on your page before you use the Gradient tool. After selecting an object, click and drag over it with the gradient tool to determine the direction of the gradient. The longer you drag, the longer the gradient. For an abrupt transition between colors in the gradient click and drag over a shorter distance.

Navigation Tools

InDesign provides multiple tools for navigating through your document.

Grabber Hand

You can use the Hand tool (press H) to scroll around a page or even between pages. When using other tools, you can temporarily access the Hand temporarily by holding down the Option/Alt key followed by the space bar.

Zoom

Use the Zoom tool (press Z) to change the view magnification in your document window. Pressing Command/Ctrl-spacebar temporarily activates the Zoom tool when working with another tool. Add the Option/Alt key to decrease the page magnification.

Determining Color Selections

The Tools palette also lets you control how InDesign applies fills and strokes. You can reset the currently selected colors to the default colors (press D), identify whether the text or frame is being modified, and even apply the last used solid color, gradient or no color from the Tools palette. We discuss colors and how to create and apply them in more detail in Chapter 38.

The last two buttons in the Tools palette control the Preview mode, which we discuss in the next chapter.

4

Views and Navigation

InDesign includes a number of nifty, efficient and innovative navigation tools that make it unnecessary to use those clunky scroll bars to move within your documents.

Document Window Navigation

InDesign displays the current page magnification in the lower-left corner of your document window (see Figure 4-1). You can select from any of the preset magnification levels (in the popup menu next to the magnification setting), which range from five percent to 4000 percent. You can also enter a magnification value other than the presets (press Command-Option-5/Ctrl-Alt-5 to jump to that field), then press the Enter or Return key for your value to be accepted.

Figure 4-1
The document window navigation panel

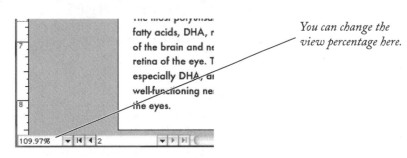

You can change the view percentage here.

Zoom Tool

You can quickly select the zoom tool by pressing Z on your keyboard when the text cursor isn't active or selecting it in the Toolbar.

Click and drag around objects to be magnified. This allows you to avoid having to click multiple times to increase the magnification. To zoom out with this tool, hold down the Option/Alt key while clicking the mouse.

You can temporarily activate this tool by pressing the Command/Ctrl key and the spacebar together. Add the Option/Alt key to this combination to reduce the magnification.

Useful Key Commands for Navigating

InDesign provides several key commands to help you achieve the optimum page magnification. Use Command-0/Ctrl-0 to fit the current active page into your window. InDesign is also able to fit the active spread into the window, not just the active page: press Command-Option-0/Ctrl-Alt-0.

You can easily access a 100-percent zoom by selecting Command-1/ Ctrl-1, a 200-percent view by selecting Command-2/Ctrl-2, and a 400-percent view with Command-4/Ctrl-4. Switch between your last two zoom levels by pressing Command-Option-2/Ctrl-Alt-2. Of course you can also access most of these commands under the View menu.

Hand Tool

The Hand tool (H from your keyboard) allows you to "grab" a portion of the page and move your view by dragging the page within the document window. This tool provides one of the most efficient ways to move around a document page because it lets you move both vertically and horizontally at the same time. You can temporarily activate this tool while you are using another tool by holding down the Option/Alt key plus the spacebar.

Moving Between Pages

You are able to easily move between the pages in your document using a variety of tools.

Pages Palette

The Pages palette provides an icon representing each page in your document (see Figure 4-2). You can double-click on a page icon to move to that page. The page number that you are currently viewing appears bold in the Pages palette.

Figure 4-2
The Pages palette

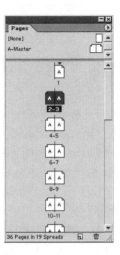

Document Window Navigation

The current page and zoom magnification is always listed in the navigation panel in the lower-left corner of the document window. Move to a specific page by clicking the down arrow at the right of the page number and then select a page from the pop-up list (see Figure 4-3). To move forward or backward within the document by clicking the right or left facing arrows.

The Navigator Palette

InDesign's Navigator palette shows a tiny representation of an entire page or the entire document. A red box in the palette identifies the area which is currently visible on screen. At the bottom of the palette, you can use the sliding triangle to zoom in or zoom out of the page by dragging it right

Figure 4-3
Selecting a page from the navigation panel

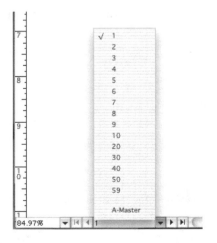

or left. Use this palette to efficiently navigate oversized documents such as posters and gate-folds.

Showing and Hiding Page Elements

InDesign lets you show and hide your page guides and ruler guides with a single command: Show/Hide Guides from the View menu (or press Command-;/Ctrl-;). This command hides or shows the ruler and page guides. InDesign lets you independently hide or show other page properties, such as frame edges, baseline grid, and also master page items.

Frame Edges

By using the Hide Frame Edges command from the View menu (Command-H/Ctrl-H), you can often better position an item near a guide without the frame interfering with the view.

Baseline Grid

If you create multiple-column documents you probably should be using the baseline grid, which places horizontal lines across your document which you can use for alignment. Make the lines visible from the View menu by select Show Baseline Grid (or hide it by selecting Hide Baseline Grid). The keyboard shortcut is Command-Option-'/Ctrl-Alt-' (single quote). The grid settings are based on the values in the Grids panel of the Preferences dialog box.

Text Threads

InDesign makes it easy to see which text frames are linked to each other. Turn on Show Text Threads from the View menu (Command-Option-Y/Ctrl-Alt-Y). You can hide the threads with the same command. Threads are visible when you've selected a text frame with the Selection tools.

Document Grid

InDesign has a grid you can display or hide by selecting Show/Hide Document Grid from the View menu (or press Command-'/Ctrl-'). The document grid can take the place of having to build your own guides. You can control the document grid settings in the Preferences dialog box.

Master Items

InDesign provides an innovative option which allows you to show or hide master page items. You can use this to easily determine what items are master page items versus local, individual page items. Select Display Master Items from the View menu.

Preview Modes

The Preview Mode hides every non-printing page element (frames, guides, grids, and so on) in one quick step and places the document on a neutral gray background. Click the Preview Mode button at the bottom of the Tools palette (or press W—when you are not editing text, of course). Click the Normal View button or press W again to switch back to normal viewing mode. Click and hold on the Preview Mode button to access Bleed Mode, which displays the document and any bleed or use the Slug Mode to display the document, bleed and slug areas of the document.

Managing Palettes

Adobe InDesign has a great many palettes, which makes it important to know how to quickly access, hide, and manage them.

Palette Key Commands

Many palettes have their own keyboard shortcuts. These make the palettes visible and activate their first field. Or, if the palettes are displayed, the shortcut hides them. Once the first field of the palette is active, you can enter a specific value and then use the Tab and Shift-Tab keystrokes to move between fields.

Minimize Palettes

Minimize your palettes (Figure 4-4) by clicking the Grow Window/ Maximize button at the top of the palette. You can also double-click on the name of a palette to have the palette expand or contract its view. Some palettes sport three views, so double-clicking on the palette name provides you with an expanded view, a reduced view, and a view where only the palette name is displayed.

Combining and Docking Palettes

Because you are working with so many more palettes with InDesign it is important to customize your workspace to efficiently find what you need.

Figure 4-4
A minimized palette

By default, many palettes are attached to the right side of the document window. Clicking the name tab of a palette that is attached to the side of the window causes the palette to slide out and become fully visible—or if it is already expanded, to hide the palette and only show its name.

Palettes that are attached to the side of the window can be positioned anywhere on the screen by clicking and dragging. You can also customize the grouping of various palettes so that the palettes you need are positioned together in a palette group, or separated so that you can view them independently. For example, the Swatches and Character Styles palettes are combined by default, but by clicking and dragging the title tab of either one of these palettes you can separate them. To combine palettes that are separate, click and drag a palette (by its title tab) on top of any other palette (see Figure 4-5).

You can also join palettes together so they are "docked" by dragging the title tab of one palette over the bottom edge of another–wait until the palette's bottom edge highlights before letting go. When palettes are combined or docked, they'll always hide and show at the same time.

Figure 4-5
Combined and docked palettes

 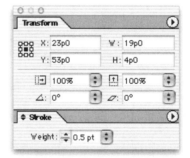

Using Workspaces

Workspaces provide a handy tool for managing the dizzying array of palettes. By creating a workspace you can save the position of all open palettes on your screen, making it easy to access them again. To save the positions of all open palettes as a workspace choose Windows>Workspace>Save Workspace. To activate a workspace, choose the name of the workspace you wish to use from that same submenu.

Use the Control Palette

When editing text you can use the Character palette, the Paragraph palette, the Character Styles palette, and the Paragraph Styles palette—or replace all those with the Control palette. The Control palette is a versatile palette that combines many of the common attributes that are typically found by using individual palettes. By default, the Control palette is attached to the top of the document window, just below the menu bars. When editing text, you can choose to edit either Paragraph or Character attributes in this palette by clicking on the appropriate buttons on the left side of the palette (or press Command-Option-7/Ctrl-Alt-7 to swap the views).

When objects are selected using one of the selection tools, the Control palette can also be used in place of the Transform palette and the Stroke palette, as it displays positioning and size information along with stroke (border) options.

Making Objects Non-printing

You can make objects non-printing (that is, they appear on screen but don't print out) with InDesign. There are many reasons you might want non-printing objects in your document. For instance, you might want to add a note you want someone else handling the document to see, but which you don't want to appear when you print out the page that it's on.

To make an object non-printing with InDesign, open the Attributes palette (from the Window menu), select the object, and turn on the Nonprinting checkbox (see Figure 4-6).

Figure 4-6
The Attributes palette

This checkbox sets the nonprinting attribute.

InDesign also lets you preview the printing status of objects by selecting the Preview mode button on the Tools palette, or pressing W (when you don't have a text insertion point). Non-printing objects disappear in any of the preview modes.

You can also have InDesign suppress the printout (not print) all pictures in a document. Do this in the Print dialog box by selecting None from the Images menu on the Graphics panel.

Tip: You can disable printing for every object on a layer by Option/Alt-clicking on a layer in the Layers palette (to select all the objects on that layer) and then, in the Attributes palette, turn select the Nonprinting checkbox.

5

Keyboard Shortcuts and Context Menus

Context-sensitive menus, or just "context menus" for short, can help you save a tremendous amount of time by providing a menu that changes depending on what or where you click your mouse. More specifically, the menu changes based upon what is selected and where your mouse is positioned when you right-click (Windows) or Control-click (Macintosh). Here are some of our favorite timesaving options that you can use.

- Context menus when a page guide is selected let you copy, paste or move the guides. You can even change the guides color by choosing Ruler Guides.

- You can also use context menus on the document ruler (the rulers at the top and left of the document window) to switch ruler measurements.

- You can reduce or enlarge frame sizes with the Fit Frame to Content option. This works with both text and graphic frames (see Figure 5-1).

- Use the Fit Content to Frame to proportionally or disproportionately cause graphic content inside of a frame to enlarge or reduce to fit into the frame in which it resides.

- You can apply a drop shadow or feather to an object. When working with picture frames, remember to take care in what is selected; if you use the Direct Select tool, you may select the image rather than the picture frame.

User Interface

Figure 5-1
Use the context menu to save time applying borders or fitting graphics within a frame.

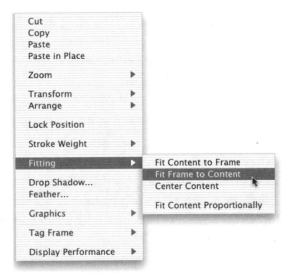

Keyboard Shortcuts

With InDesign you can customize the keyboard shortcuts to change existing keyboard commands or add new commands if none exist.

Finding Shortcuts

Keyboard shortcuts are typically listed adjacent to the commands in the menus. Additionally, many keyboard shortcuts from other Adobe software work in InDesign, too. For example, the zoom in and zoom out shortcuts (Command-=/Ctrl-= and Command-hyphen/Ctrl-hyphen) work in all of the Adobe publishing applications.

Printing Shortcuts

Perhaps the best way to learn the keyboard shortcuts is to print a complete list of all the current keyboard shortcuts. To do this, select Keyboard Shortcuts from the Edit menu and then click the Show Set button (see Figure 5-2). InDesign saves a file of these shortcuts on your hard disk and then opens it with the system's default text editor (like TextEdit or Windows Notepad). This file, which you can print, contains a complete list of all possible keyboard shortcuts.

Customizing Shortcuts

It's not hard to customize the keyboard commands used by InDesign, but you do need to take some care to get it right. Here's what you do.

1. Select Keyboard Shortcuts from the Edit menu, then choose the Set you want to modify (or click New Set to make your own). You can alter the Default set, but we don't recommend it, as it's nice to be able to go back to the original settings.

2. Choose a subject from the Product Area popup menu, and then choose the command you want to change from the Commands portion of the window.

3. After selecting a command to be modified, InDesign displays the current keyboard shortcut in the Current Shortcuts field. You can eliminate a current shortcut (there may be more than one, each with a different context) by clicking the Remove shortcut without assigning a new shortcut.

4. If you want to add a new shortcut, first choose from the four choices in the Context popup menu: Alerts/Dialogs, Text, Default, XML, and Tables. This controls when the shortcut will be active. For instance, if you choose Tables, then the keyboard shortcut will only function when your text cursor is in a table.

5. Finally, click in the New Shortcut portion of the window, enter the keystroke you want, and click the Assign button. Your new shortcut should then be listed in the Current Shortcuts portion of the window. When done assigning keyboard shortcuts, click the OK button.

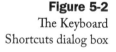

Figure 5-2
The Keyboard
Shortcuts dialog box

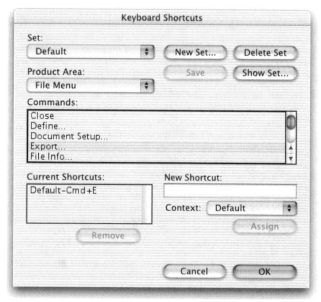

PART 3

Building Pages

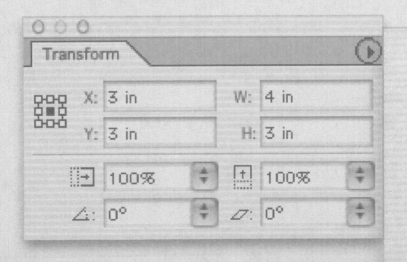

6

Creating Frames

The basic elements of an InDesign page are the same as they are in a QuarkXPress or PageMaker page—boxes, lines and text paths. But since you're now working in a new "country," you have to learn the language of your new land, which is a little different than the kingdom you know.

Understanding the Lingo

InDesign calls the basic elements of a page *frames*. In PageMaker, when working with text and graphics, using frames is optional, but in InDesign they're required. As in XPress, frames (called *boxes* in XPress) are used as the container for text or graphics, or they may have no content at all.

QuarkXPress uses the word *frame* to mean the border around a box. It calls the thickness of a frame its *width*. When you want to change the background, you change the *box color*. InDesign and PageMaker, on the other hand, follows Illustrator's terminology, and calls the border of a frame the *stroke*. When you change the thickness of a stroke, you change its *stroke weight*. Similarly, when a frame has a background color, InDesign and PageMaker calls it the *fill*.

The other basic element of a QuarkXPress or PageMaker page is a line. InDesign calls these—and the edges around a frame—*paths*.

Flexibility with Frames

When you work with QuarkXPress boxes, you have one workflow: First, you draw a text box or a picture box as a placeholder, then you fill it with content. You can do that in InDesign, but you can also create frames on-the-fly.

Placeholder Frames

When you want to use the placeholder method, you can use InDesign's frame tools (see Figure 6-1). There are three basic tools to create a frame in the shape of a rectangle, an ellipse, and a regular polygon. (We'll show you how create squares, circles and stars from these tools in Chapter 8. And you can make fancier boxes with corner effects, which we describe in Chapter 9.)

Figure 6-1
The Rectangle,
Ellipse, and Polygon
Frame tools

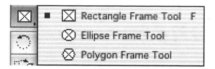

Note that there aren't separate frame tools for text and pictures, as there are in XPress; you use the same tool to create either a text or picture placeholder. By default, these tools create graphic placeholders (also called "picture frames"), indicated by the "X" in them (see Figure 6-2). However, you can turn them into text frames by clicking in them with the Type tool or selecting the frame and choosing Text from the Content submenu (under the Object menu). You can recognize text frames by their in and out ports, used for connecting the frames. Unassigned frames have neither an "X" or ports.

Frames On-the-Fly

InDesign also offers the choice of creating frames on-the-fly. To place a graphic or text when no frame has been created, you can simply choose Place from the File menu (or press Command-D/Ctrl-D). After selecting a graphic or text file to place, you'll see the loaded "Place gun" cursor (see Figure 6-3). If you click, InDesign automatically creates a frame and places the graphic or text in it, at the point where you click. You can also click-and-drag on the page with the loaded graphics cursor, which places the picture inside a frame with one corner where you clicked and another corner where you let go of the mouse button.

You can also make text frames on the fly by dragging out a rectangular frame with the Type tool. After dragging out the shape, the text insertion point is flashing, ready to accept your text.

Figure 6-2
Three selected frames
with graphic, text,
and unassigned
content

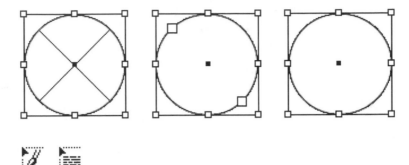

Figure 6-3
The loaded graphics
and text cursors

Dragging and Copying Shortcuts

InDesign has two more frame creating tricks up its sleeve. First, if nothing is selected when you paste graphics or text from the clipboard (select Paste from the Edit menu or press Command-V/Ctrl-V), InDesign creates a frame in the center of your current page. We discuss copying graphics from Adobe Illustrator and Macromedia Freehand in Chapter 28. Be warned, however, that when you copy a bitmapped image, it is becomes an embedded object and is not linked to a file on disk (we don't recommend doing this).

The second trick is a truly amazing way to add text or graphics to a page: You can select one or more text or graphic files on the Windows or Macintosh system desktop or in Windows Explorer and drag the files into InDesign! On the Macintosh, drag the files into an InDesign window until you see a black outline around window, then release the mouse. In Windows, drag the files over a minimized InDesign window and, when the window opens, release the mouse. InDesign creates a frame for each file (they're stacked if you're dragging several files), and the frames are linked to their external files. What a time saver!

If you drag a single image or text file on top of an empty frame, InDesign places the file into that frame. You can also drag images from Photoshop's File Browser window into InDesign.

7

Tools for Selecting

While it may seem obvious, before you can work with objects on a page, you have to select them. While QuarkXPress has the Item and Content tools for selecting and PageMaker has the Pointer tool, InDesign uses three tools: The Selection tool, the Direct Selection tool, and the Type tool. Selecting objects in InDesign is one of the most frustrating tasks for someone used to the way XPress or PageMaker does it.

The Selection tool (press V) selects an entire object; you can also use it to move or resize a frame or path (see Figure 7-1). The Direct Selection tool (press A) selects or edits *part* of an object, such as a single point on a path or a graphic frame's content. At first glance it appears that the Selection tool is like XPress's Item tool and the Direct Selection tool is like XPress's Content tool, but the similarity breaks down in several ways. For instance, to select or edit the content of a text frame, you must use the Type tool (press T). (Because text is handled so differently than other objects, we'll discuss the use of this tool in Part 4.)

Bounding Boxes and Anchor Points

InDesign is engineered from the ground up to allow shape editing. The appearance of a selected frame changes depending on the tool you are

Figure 7-1
The Selection,
Direct Selection, and
Type tools

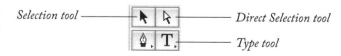

Selection tool ——————— Direct Selection tool

——— Type tool

working with. When the Selection tool is active, a selected path or frame shows eight bounding box handles (one on each corner, one on each side; see Figure 7-2). A solid, non-printing center point also appears which is handy for selecting objects that have no content.

When the Direct Selection tool is active, you see the *anchor points* which make up the shape of the path or frame (see Figure 7-3). A non-printing center point is also displayed. We'll describe how to edit the shape of frames in the next chapter.

If you're working with the Selection tool, you can select more than one frame or path by Shift-clicking; you'll see the bounding boxes of each selected object. If you're working with the Direct Selection tool, you can Shift-click to choose more than one anchor point in frames and paths or Option-click to select all the points on the path. With either tool, to deselect an object or anchor point, just Shift-click again.

Dragging with the Selection tool selects any objects whose shape falls within the marqueed area, no matter how little they are included. Marqueeing with the Direct Selection tool chooses any anchor points within the selection rectangle.

Lastly, you can select all of the objects on a page or spread by choosing Select All from the Edit menu (Command-A/Ctrl-A). InDesign also has a handy deselect command—Deselect All from the same menu (Command-Shift-A/Ctrl-Shift-A). We use Deselect All very frequently, such as before creating a new color in the Colors palette (so that the new color won't be applied to any accidentally-selected objects).

Figure 7-2
Path and frame
with the Selection
tool active

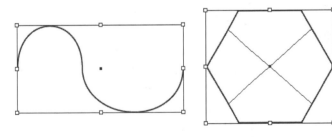

Figure 7-3
The same objects
with the Direct
Selection tool active

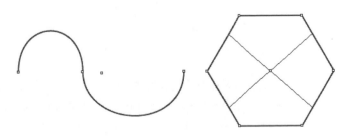

8

Creating and Editing Shapes

Now that you know how InDesign works with frames and paths, and how to select them, we'd better show you how to create some. As you might expect, there are tools available to create simple, freeform and precise shapes. Later in this chapter, we'll also explain how to reshape these objects once you've made them.

Simple Shapes

Simple shapes are the ones we create the most, so InDesign has specialized tools for making specific shapes.

Line Tool

Unlike QuarkXPress or PageMaker, there is only one tool dedicated to creating straight lines in InDesign. (You can also create creates lines with the Pencil or Pen tools, described below.) When you finish dragging with the Line tool, you'll see the bounding box of the line (unless the line is horizontal or vertical, in which case you only see the two end points). Dragging while holding down the Shift key is the equivalent of drawing with XPress's Orthogonal Line or PageMaker's Constrained Line tool—it constrains your line horizontally or vertically. Plus, if you hold down the Option/Alt key while you drag, you can draw the line from the center.

Rectangle, Ellipse, and Polygon Tools

When you want to make a background tint rectangle—a frame with no content—the Rectangle tool (press M; see Figure 8-1) is the one for you.

Figure 8-1

The Rectangle, Ellipse, and Polygon tools

You can also use the Ellipse (press L) and Polygon tools to make content-less frames. What about a rounded corner rectangle? We show how to make these in Chapter 9 using corner effects.

There are several modifier keys which work with these three tools:

- Holding down the Shift key constrains the shape to have the same height and width.

- Holding down the Option/Alt key draws the shape from the center.

- Holding down Shift-Option/Shift-Alt draws a square or circular shape from the center.

- Holding down the spacebar when drawing lets you move the shape while still drawing it.

The Polygon tool is even more versatile—you can even use it to draw starbursts! After selecting this tool, double-click on the tool icon in the Tools palette to open the Polygon Settings dialog box. Here you can set the number of sides for a polygon. The default Star Inset is 0% which creates a polygon, but if you choose a positive value, you create stars. Increasing the percentage moves the inner vertices of the star inward, creating a spikier star.

Freeform Shapes

As with QuarkXPress, InDesign offers two types of tools to create Bézier shapes—freeform and precise tools. If you haven't learned to use the Pen tool in another application, the freeform tools are the easiest to use. Let's take a look at the three freeform drawing tools first.

Pencil Tool

The Pencil tool (press N) works analogously to QuarkXPress's Freehand Box and Line tools (see Figure 8-2). To create a line, you simply draw with it like you would on a piece of paper. But InDesign's Pencil tool not only draws, it redraws: if, after drawing a line, you draw over part of the line, InDesign deletes from that point to the end and the redraws using the new path you specified. If you want to use the Pencil to create a frame instead of a line, draw the shape, then hold down the Option/Alt key and a tiny circle cursor appears. Release the mouse button first, then the key, and you make a closed shape.

Smooth Tool

You can use the Smooth tool to smooth out a freeform shape. Dragging the Smooth tool over a path reduces the angularity of curves (helping to compensate for your shaking hand!) and produces a curve with fewer anchor points.

In InDesign, you can control how accurately the Pencil and Smooth tools follow your mouse movements by double-clicking on each tool, opening the Pencil Tool Preferences dialog box or a similar dialog box for the Smooth tool.

Figure 8-2
The Pencil, Smooth, and Erase tools

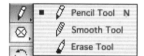

Erase Tool

Finally, drag with the Erase tool to delete part of the any path or frame you create. It works like a real world eraser, erasing anchor points and the line segments between them.

Precise Shapes with the Pen Tool

To be honest, when we're creating a frame or path, we always use the Pen tool (press P; see Figure 8-3), not the freeform tools. The reason: Despite the freeform controls we just told you about, it's almost impossible to create a precise path with those tools. InDesign uses a Pen tool and other path editing tools which are similar to those in XPress, and virtually identical to those in Illustrator or Photoshop. If you've learned to use the Pen tool in another Adobe product, you're home free! This section doesn't pretend to be a complete course in making precise paths (*Real World InDesign CS* covers the drawing tools in more detail). Instead we'll focus here on just the basics.

First, a little terminology review when you're working with precise paths (see Figure 8-4): The tiny squares which control the shape of a curve are called *anchor points*. InDesign uses *smooth points* and *corner points* like QuarkXPress, but it doesn't have *symmetrical points* (they exist in InDesign, but there's no special control to create them automatically like there is in XPress). The handles that extend out from anchor points are called

Figure 8-3
The Pen tool and associated tools

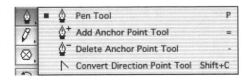

Figure 8-4
Curve terminology

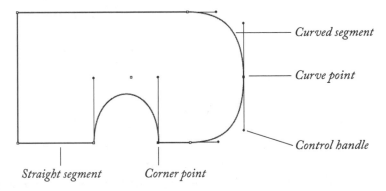

control handles. Smooth points have two handles which move in unison around an anchor point. Corner points have either one, two, or no control handles, and their handles move independently of each other. The lines which connect the anchor points are called *segments,* which can be either curved or straight.

Similarities and Differences

While QuarkXPress uses different tools to create Bézier lines, text boxes, etc., InDesign has only one Pen tool. Creating most paths with the Pen tool works the same as in XPress:

- Clicking makes straight segments.
- Shift-clicking constrains line segments to 45- or 90-degree angles.
- Dragging creates smooth points.
- Shift-dragging constrains control handles to 45° or 90° angles.
- Moving over a path starting point always closes the path (in Quark-XPress this only works with boxes, not lines).
- Clicking on the Pen tool after drawing a path lets you end one path begin a new one.

Reshaping Paths and Frames

InDesign uses the Direct Selection tool and several other dedicated tools for reshaping and editing the paths and frames which you've created with the Pen tool or any other method. You can use them immediately on any object without having to go into a special editing mode like QuarkXPress forces you to do.

Direct Selection Tool

Use the Direct Selection tool, not the Pen tool, to edit paths or frames. You can even use it while drawing: With the Pen tool selected, holding down the Command/Ctrl key gives you temporary access to this tool so you can move an anchor point as you're drawing.

Add Anchor Point Tool

The Add Anchor Point tool, hidden under the Pen tool, is a tool dedicated to adding anchor points to an existing path or frame. When using this tool to add an anchor point, simply select a path or frame and move over a straight or curved segment. When you see the small + cursor, click the tool. However, we never actually select this tool. It's much faster just to use the Pen tool. Whenever you move the Pen over a selected path or frame and see the same + cursor, clicking adds a point.

Delete Anchor Point Tool

The Delete Anchor Point tool, also hidden under the Pen tool, deletes anchor points on a frame or path. When you move this tool over an anchor point, you'll see a small – (minus) cursor. Just click the tool to delete the anchor point. You can do the same thing with the Pen tool when you move over an anchor point.

Convert Direction Point Tool

The last in this group of tools hidden under the Pen tool is the Convert Direction Point tool. It's a very versatile tool which changes corner points into smooth points and vice versa, and which you can use to manipulate handles. This tool has three modes:

- Clicking over a smooth point turns it into a corner point (it sucks in the control handles).

- Dragging from a corner point drags out control handles, making it a smooth point.

- Dragging on the control handles of a smooth point converts it to a corner point with independent handles.

Scissors Tool

Finally, almost as an afterthought, InDesign has hidden one more path editing tool, the Scissors tool (press C; see Figure 8-5), under the Gradient tool, of all places!

You can use the Scissors tool to split a path or a frame, whether or not the frame has any content. When you click on a segment of a path or frame, InDesign creates two anchor points at the cut, one on top of the other. If you want to cut a frame in two, you need to cut it twice; otherwise, you'll just create an single path which has a gap.

Figure 8-5
The Scissors tool

Pathfinder Commands

InDesign CS also offers commands for combining shapes. These are similar to the Merge commands in QuarkXPress, or the Pathfinder features in Illustrator. You can find these commands by selecting the Pathfinder palette (choose Pathfinder from the Window menu). You can also choose the commands from the Pathfinder submenu under the Object menu. The commands work by selecting two or more shapes and choosing a Pathfinder command.

There are five Pathfinder commands:

- The Add command combines multiple shapes into one shape.
- The Subtract command subtracts shapes in front from the one in back.
- The Intersect command chooses what is in common between multiple shapes.
- The Exclude Overlap command excludes overlapping shape areas.
- The Minus Back command subtracts shapes in back from the shape which is in front.

The Pathfinder features combine shapes into a *compound path*—a shape made up of two or more *subpaths*, which usually contains holes when one subpath is contained within another. For instance, when you convert text to outlines, you get a compound path made of individual paths (letter shapes). You can also create a compound path by selecting multiple objects and choosing Make from the Compound Paths submenu (under the Object menu). The objects will be combined into one compound path.

9

Fills and Strokes

As we mentioned in Chapter 6, InDesign and PageMaker use a different dialect than QuarkXPress when it comes to describing page objects: QuarkXPress works with a box's background color, while InDesign lets you manipulate a frame's fill color. What XPress calls a box's frame InDesign calls a stroke. Every object on a page has a fill and a stroke, even if the color is "None" (transparent) or the stroke is set to zero points.

In InDesign, you usually change an object's fill or stroke color with the Swatches palette. We'll discuss in detail the use of the Swatches palette and other methods of applying color in Part 8, *Color and Transparency*. To change an object's stroke width, you use the Stroke or Control palette.

The part that confuses many XPress users is that before you apply a color to an object, you have to choose whether the color should apply to the stroke or the fill. The easiest way to select between the fill and stroke attributes is at the bottom of the Tools palette (see Figure 9-1). The two largest buttons select the fill and stroke: Clicking the square one selects the fill attributes; choosing the outlined one selects the stroke attributes. The one in front is the active attribute. You can swap between the two by pressing the letter X when not editing text. These fill and stroke icons also appear in the Swatches and Color palettes.

Clicking the small icon below the fill/stroke controls (or pressing D) returns you to the default—a black stroke with no fill. If you apply the color to the stroke when you meant to apply it to the fill (or vice versa), don't fret: just press Shift-X to swap them.

Note that when you select a text frame with the Selection or Direct Select tool, you have to make one more choice here: Click the Formatting

Figure 9-1
Fill and Stroke controls on the Tools and Swatches palettes

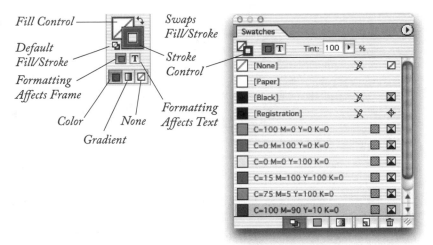

Fill Control

Default Fill/Stroke

Formatting Affects Frame

Color   *None*

Gradient

Swaps Fill/Stroke

Stroke Control

Formatting Affects Text

Building Pages

Affects Frame or the Formatting Affects Text button in order to choose which of the two (frame or text) will have the color applied to it. Also, below these buttons are controls that let you apply the last used color (press period when not editing text) or gradient (press comma), or to apply "None" (no color; press /).

Fills

The fills of InDesign's frames can be transparent (None), a color, or a gradient. However, while XPress or PageMaker don't let you fill paths, InDesign does. If you haven't closed a path, the fill still appears as though the path were a closed frame. (If the path is more complex, the fill will be less predictable.)

InDesign even lets you fill your text with a color, a gradient, or None (no color). A gradient (blend) applied to text is based on the whole width or height of the frame; not just the text itself (see Chapter 38).

Strokes

InDesign, QuarkXPress, and PageMaker offer similar ways of applying a stroke. However, InDesign not only lets you apply a width and color, you can even apply a gradient to any path—even text. And when you apply a stroke to text, it stays editable.

Note that, unlike the other two applications, the weight of a stroke in InDesign can be centered either on the path's center, or on the inside, or the outside of the path (see Figure 9-2). The choice is made on Stroke

Figure 9-2
Stroking a path,
InDesign CS can
center on the center,
the inside or the
outside.

palette with the Align Stroke buttons. (However, this doesn't apply to stroked text, unless you convert the text to outlines first.)

The Stroke Palette

Although you can assign a stroke thickness and type from the Control palette, the real control center for working with strokes in InDesign is the Stroke palette (see Figure 9-3). To see all the choices for the Stroke palette, choose Show Options from the palette menu.

The Weight control lets you either choose from a popup menu of preset stroke weights or type in an arbitrary weight from 0 to 800 points.

InDesign borrows some stroke controls—notably *Cap* styles and *Miter* styles—from Adobe Illustrator. The Cap style affects the appearance of both ends of an open path (see Figure 9-4). The cap style choices are:

- A *butt cap*, which creates square ends (the default).

- A *round cap*, which creates rounded ends.

- A *projecting cap*, which extends the ends of the path beyond the end points by half the thickness of the stroke.

The Join styles control the appearance of a path at a corner point (not smooth curves; see Figure 9-5). There are also three choices:

- A miter join (the default) creates a crisp, pointed corner. However, InDesign may crop the corner, depending on the Miter Limit value.

- A *round join* creates a rounded corner.

- A *bevel join* creates cuts off the end of the point on the corner.

Dashes, Stripes, and Path End Shapes

The bottom section of the Stroke palette gives you the controls for working with preset dashes, dotted lines and stripes, and path end shapes (like arrowheads). There are also controls for Gap Color and Gap Tint.

Figure 9-3
The Stroke palette

Building Pages

Figure 9-4
Cap styles

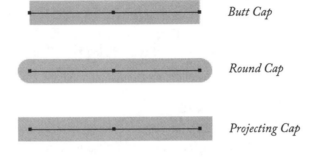

Butt Cap

Round Cap

Projecting Cap

Figure 9-5
Join styles

Miter Join   *Round Join*   *Bevel Join*

The Type popup menu lets you choose between different path styles. You can choose between a solid path, preset stripes (like Thick-Thin), and dashed and dotted paths. For dashes, you'll get the most control if you select the Dashed choice. Then the appearance of the palette changes to allow you to enter dash and gap values. You might use this to create the dashed path for a special coupon border, for example.

When you choose a dashed, dotted or striped stroke, you also get the choice of selecting a different color to fill the gaps in the stroke, called the Gap Color, and a tint of that color, called the Gap Tint.

The Start and End popup menus have choices for path endings for the beginning point and end point of a path. You can choose between arrowheads, bars, circles, and so on, but the choices aren't editable.

Stroke Styles

InDesign CS introduces the ability to create your own stroke styles, similar to the way the Dashes and Stripes editor works in QuarkXPress. You can choose between creating a dashed, dotted or striped stroke. To do this, choose Stroke Styles from the Stroke palette flyout menu. In the Stroke Styles dialog box (Figure 9-6), click New to create a new stroke style. Enter a name for the style, and choose a type (Dash, Dotted or Stripe) from the popup menu.

You'll see one of three options for editing the style, depending on the type you choose. You can either drag in the ruler window to visually create the style, or you can enter numeric values which define the style. When you are through editing the style, click OK. The new stroke will be added to the list in the Stroke Styles dialog box. There are also controls there for editing, deleting, loading and saving stroke styles.

Corner Effects

While InDesign's Tools palette only shows three built-in frame shape tools—Rectangle, Ellipse and Polygon—you can actually easily create any of the other shapes QuarkXPress or PageMaker has to offer. The key is to select Corner Effects from the Object menu. The Corner Effects dialog box lets you apply five different preset corner effects to your path or frame.

The most common choice to create a Rounded corner effect, but you can also use it to create fancier choices—Inverse Rounded, Bevel, Inset or Fancy.

Figure 9-6
Stroke Styles

10

Moving and Transforming Objects

Apart from selecting objects or editing text, most of us probably spend more time moving and transforming objects on the page than any other activity. That makes this is a particularly important chapter.

The Transform and Control Palettes

QuarkXPress uses a Measurement palette to move or transform objects, and PageMaker uses a Control palette. InDesign CS lets you move and resize objects with either the Transform palette or the Control palette. These palettes provide two essential functions: First, they provide precise data about an object's position, size, angle, and so on. Second, they provide the ability to numerically transform these attributes (see Figure 10-1).

When an object is selected, the values shown are in the current ruler units (based on the settings in the Preferences dialog box) and are relative to the position of the ruler origin. InDesign's default ruler origin is the upper left corner of the page, the same as in XPress and PageMaker.

Setting the Transformation Origin
InDesign—unlike XPress, but like PageMaker—is flexible and lets you pick the transformation point. This can be useful when you'd like to resize a frame from its center, for example.

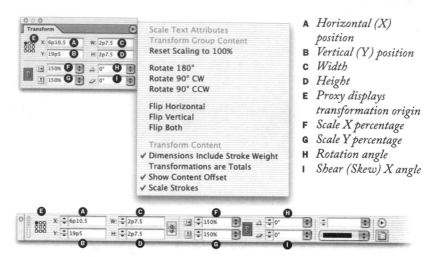

Figure 10-1
The Transform and
Control palettes

A *Horizontal (X)
position*
B *Vertical (Y) position*
C *Width*
D *Height*
E *Proxy displays
transformation origin*
F *Scale X percentage*
G *Scale Y percentage*
H *Rotation angle*
I *Shear (Skew) X angle*

The Transform and Control palettes add a small icon called the *proxy*, where you can select the transformation origin. Clicking a point on the proxy sets the origin.

When using the Scale, Rotate and Shear tools (described later in this chapter) the proxy point also shows up in the document window itself—you can see the transformation point as a small nonprinting target icon. You can use these tools to drag the transformation point someplace else—even outside the object itself. If you drag near one of the center or corner points, the proxy snaps to that point and InDesign updates the proxy icon in the Transform and Control palettes.

Pay Attention to What's Selected

When doing any kind of transformation in InDesign, pay attention to which tool you're using to select the object. Use the Selection tool to select the frame or path when you wish to transform the object and its content. You can use the Direct Selection tool to transform only part of a path or an image inside of a frame.

Moving Objects

In InDesign you can move objects on a page by dragging, by using the Transform palette, the Move dialog box, or arrow keys.

By Dragging

When you want to move a path or frame interactively, choose the object with the Selection tool and just drag it. (Holding down the Command/

Ctrl key gives you temporary access to the Selection tool if another tool is selected.) For an object that has a fill, you can drag from anywhere inside the shape. If it has a stroke, no fill, and has a content of Unassigned, you must click it on its outline to move it. If the outline is difficult to select, you can always drag an object by its nonprinting center point.

When you drag an object quickly, you'll only see the outline of your object. If you pause a second before dragging, you'll see the object previewed as you drag. (This is also true of the other transformations we describe in this chapter.)

Using the Transform Palette

A second way to move an object is by changing the values of the Position fields (X and Y) in the Control or Transform palette. Imagine that you have a text frame which is located 1 inch down and 1 inch across from the ruler origin, and you're using the upper-left proxy point. In the Transform and Control palettes, the position appears as "X = 1" in and "Y = 1" in. If you want to move the frame one inch to the right, you can change the X value to either "2 in" or "1 in + 1", then press Enter. Like XPress, InDesign can do addition, subtraction, multiplication, and division in any field that shows a number. Positive values move to the right and down, so the frame shifts one inch to the right.

Using the Move Dialog Box

InDesign borrows a third method of moving objects from Illustrator—the Move dialog box. You can get to it by selecting Move from the Transform submenu (under the Object menu). But we never do it that way. It's much faster simply to double-click the Selection tool.

Using the Arrow Keys

Finally, you can move paths and frames with the Arrow keys on the keyboard. Each time you press an Arrow key, your object moves one point, by default. Holding down the Shift key while pressing an arrow key moves by 10 points. But you can change these amounts in the Cursor Key field in the Preferences dialog box.

Resizing Objects

There are both interactive and numeric ways of resizing, or *scaling*, in InDesign. When using the numeric methods described below (the Transform palette and Scale tool), whether or not the an image inside a frame also

Figure 10-2

Transform tools in
the Tools palette

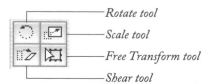

—Rotate tool

—Scale tool

—Free Transform tool

—Shear tool

changes depends on whether the Transform Content option is on or off in the Transform or Control palette's menu. This feature is turned on by default, so any transformation applies to both frame and picture; when turned off, the scaling applies only to the frame.

Dragging the Bounding Box

To resize an object interactively you need to see its bounding box, so you must select it with the Selection tool rather than the Direct Selection tool. When you drag a side handle with the Selection tool it resizes it in one dimension—horizontally or vertically. When you drag a corner handle, you resize it in both dimensions.

To maintain proportions with when resizing a path or frame, hold down the Shift key while dragging the handle. However, if you want the frame's contents to be scaled proportionally as well, hold down the Command-Shift/Ctrl-Shift keys when dragging.

Using the Transform or Control Palette

If you know exactly the new size you want the object to be, you can enter either new Height and Width values (in the W: or H: fields) and press Enter, and the object changes immediately.

If you want to scale the object to specific percentages, you can enter the new values in the Scale X Percentage and Scale Y Percentage fields, then press Enter. When the "lock" icon to the left of the fields is locked, entering one value sets the second to the same; if unlocked, the values can be set independently.

Dragging with the Scale Tool

If you're an Illustrator user, you're already familiar with the Scale tool (see Figure 10-2). InDesign's works almost identically. It has two modes—you can use it to scale by dragging, or you can use the Scale dialog to scale numerically.

To scale a selected object interactively, position the Scale tool some distance away from the transformation point (see Figure 10-3). The farther from the transformation point you start, the more control you have. Drag in the direction you want to scale the object. Dragging away from the point will make the object larger; moving closer to the point makes it smaller. Holding down the Shift key as you drag constrains to horizontal, vertical or proportional.

Using the Scale Dialog Box

To scale numerically, open the Scale dialog box. While you could choose the Scale command from the Transform submenu (under the Object menu), its much faster to simply double-click the Scale tool to open this dialog box.

Rotating

To rotate an object, InDesign gives you the Rotate tool and the Transform or Control palettes. You can also rotate with the Free Transform tool, described below. We tend to just use the palette; simply enter an angle in the Rotation field, and press Enter. You can also choose from preset rotation values found in the popup menu to the right of the field.

Dragging with the Rotate Tool

To drag with the Rotate tool, first set the point of transformation in the Transform palette proxy or by dragging the target icon anywhere on your page (it looks like a little crosshair that is, by default, in the center of the object). Then position the Rotate tool away from the transformation point (the farther away, the more control you'll have) and drag in the direction you want the object rotated. The rotation is a circular motion around the transformation point. The angle of rotation is displayed in the Transform, Control, and Info palettes. Holding down the Shift key while rotating, constrains the rotation to multiples of 45 degrees.

Figure 10-3
Dragging with the
Scale tool

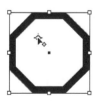

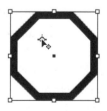

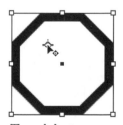

The transformation point can be moved with the Selection tool.

Dragging away from the point makes the octagon larger. The square is the outline of the scaled octagon.

The scaled octagon

Building Pages

Using the Rotate Dialog Box

If you would rather type in a rotation angle, and you have an unnatural aversion to palettes, double-click the Rotate tool, Option/Alt-click with the tool on the page, or choose Rotate from Transform submenu (in the Object menu). This opens the Rotate dialog box in which you simply enter the angle of rotation, and click OK. If you Option/Alt-click, InDesign rotates around the point where you clicked.

Flipping

In InDesign, you can flip an object with or without its content with commands on the Transform or Control palette menu: Flip Horizontal (which flips objects left-to-right, across the Y axis), Flip Vertical (which flips the object top-to-bottom, across the X axis), or Flip Both (to flip the object across both axes).

You can also flip objects with the Selection tool by dragging one of the object's bounding box handles across the object past the opposite side. In all cases, InDesign flips the object based on the point of transformation (usually based on the palette's proxy).

Skewing or Shearing

Skewing (also called shearing) is technically rotating the X and Y axes of an object differently. The result looks sort of like a 3D perspective effect. InDesign only skews horizontally, but it also fakes a vertical shear (or one on some other angle) by combining skewing and rotating.

Skewing with a Palette

To horizontally skew an object in the Transform or Control palette, enter an angle in the Shear Angle field, or choose one of the preset values in the popup menu. Both the object and its contents are slanted on the horizontal axis (unless you've turned off the Transform Content option in the palette's flyout menu). Note that a positive shear value angles the object *clockwise* (the top shifts to the right), unlike the rotation tools where a positive angle is counterclockwise.

For a vertical shear, enter the same angle in both the Shear Angle field and the Rotation field.

Using the Shear Dialog Box

You can make precise shearing transformations by opening the Shear dialog box: Double-click the Shear tool, Option/Alt-click on the page, or choose Shear from the Transform submenu (in the Object menu). Here you have options for shearing on the vertical or horizontal axis, or on any angle you want. If you Option/Alt-clicked, InDesign applies the transformation based on where you clicked.

Dragging with the Shear Tool

If you insist on doing all your transformations by dragging the cursor, you'll be happy to know you can do that with the Shear tool as well. However, unless you're careful when dragging with this tool, you may find its results wild and unpredictable.

The Free Transform Tool

InDesign has a Free Transform tool (press E), similar to the ones in Photoshop and Illustrator. The advantage of this tool is that you can quickly perform multiple transformations with the same tool. You'll need to select the object with the Selection or Direct Select tool.

- To move a selected object, click anywhere within the bounding box and move it.

- To scale a selected object, drag the bounding box handles as you would when dragging with the Selection tool. Holding down the Shift key while dragging constrains proportions. Holding down the Option/Alt key scales from the bounding box center. However, unlike the Selection tool, the content of a text frame always scales with the object (unless you selected just the frame with the Direct Selection tool).

- To rotate a selected object, drag the cursor outside the bounding box until you see a double-headed arrow cursor, then drag clockwise or counterclockwise.

- To flip the selected object over the horizontal or vertical axis, drag one of the bounding box handles across the object past the opposite side.

- To skew the selected object, start dragging a *side handle* (not a corner), then hold down the Command-Option/Ctrl-Alt keys as you drag. Also holding down the Shift key constrains vertically or horizontally.

11

Grouping, Stacking, Nesting, and Locking Objects

In the previous chapters in this part of the book, we've described how to create, edit and transform frames and paths in InDesign. This chapter focuses on some of the ways we can organize these objects when putting together a page or spread: grouping related objects, changing their *stacking order*, nesting one frame in another, and locking them in position.

Grouping

Grouping is a way to select two or more objects so you can work with them as a single object—a group. The grouping and ungrouping of objects generally works the same as in QuarkXPress or PageMaker, though there are a few differences. To group objects, first select the various paths or frames, and then select Group from the Object menu (or press Command-G/Ctrl-G). To ungroup, select the group and choose Ungroup from the Object menu (or press Command-Shift-G/Ctrl-Shift-G). Of course, you can also group multiple groups together, forming groups of groups (if you're into that sort of thing).

Where Are Your Groups?

When you select a QuarkXPress group with the Item tool, you see a dashed line around the group's rectangular bounding box. InDesign doesn't provide such a visual indicator, but you can use two cues to tell whether you've clicked on a group. First, if you see a single bounding box surrounding more than one object when you click with the Selection tool, the objects are most likely grouped. Second, see if the Ungroup command is available in the Object menu; it'll be dimmed unless you've selected a group.

Selecting the Members of a Group

You use the Direct Selection tool to select a member or members of a group so you can manipulate them without ungrouping. This works with most objects, but because InDesign also uses the Direct Selection tool to edit paths or work with picture content, you should know some tips for selecting members of a group.

- For filled paths, text frames, or straight lines, you can simply click on the object to select the member.

- If you want to select more than one member, click on one with the Direct Selection tool, then Shift-click to select the others.

- To select an entire path within a group, click once and then either click on its nonprinting center point, or hold down the Option/Alt key and click again.

- For a graphics frame, click on the edge of the frame. (If you click on the center, you'll choose the contents: the picture itself.) Press the letter V to switch to the Selection tool, and you'll see the bounding box of that object.

The Group Selection Tool

You've created a complex page with groups inside groups inside groups. You've lost track of how things are organized. And you're missing Quark-XPress's dotted line border to see where the groups are. How do you find out what's what?

There are two solutions. First, the mysterious Group Selection tool. You can't see it on the Tools palette, but it's always at your disposal. Here's how it works: In Figure 11-1, we've created two groups—the circles and the squares—then we grouped these two groups together. Click once with the Direct Selection tool on a path segment (not anchor point). Then, to get the Group Selection tool, hold down the Option/Alt key (the + cursor shows you have the right tool) and click again. This time the entire path is selected. A third Option/Alt-click shows the first level of grouping. A fourth click shows the second level of grouping. Each time you click with the Group Selection tool, you get the next hierarchy of grouping.

Figure 11-1
Clicking through
the groups

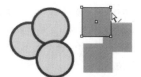

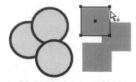

*1. First click with the Direct
Selection to choose the path segment.*

*2. Holding Option/Alt, the second
click selects the complete path.*

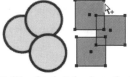

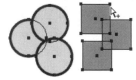

3. The third click selects the first group.

4. Finally, the top level of grouping.

The Select Container and Select Content buttons in the Control palette do a very similar thing: selecting "down" into a group or "up" to select a group of objects.

Nesting

In InDesign, any object—text frame, graphics frame or path—can contain another object. This concept is called *nesting*, and it can give you great freedom in combining objects on your page.

To nest an object in another object, just choose the first object, which we'll call the "child," with the Selection tool, and Copy or Cut it to the Clipboard. Then select the second object, which we'll call the "parent," and choose Paste Into (not Paste!) from the Edit menu. You can only nest one object in another object at a time, but a group of objects counts as a single object—so if you want to nest more than one object in a frame, group them first.

Stacking Order

InDesign lets you stack objects on top of each other in two ways: stacking order and layers. We'll discuss layers and the Layers palette in Chapter 13. Here we cover stacking order, the vertical arrangement of objects within a layer.

InDesign has the same four stacking commands for controlling the vertical order of page objects as in XPress and PageMaker (you can find these commands in the Arrange submenu, under the Object menu):

- Bring to Front—or press Command-Shift-] / Ctrl-Shift-]

- Bring Forward—or press Command-] / Ctrl-]
- Send Backward—or press Command-[/ Ctrl-[
- Send to Back—or press Command-Shift-[/ Ctrl-Shift-[

Another fast way of selecting these commands is to use the context menu: You'll see these same features if you right-click on an object in Windows, or Control-click it on the Macintosh.

Selecting Object Controls

InDesign also has some controls for selecting objects which are stacked, nested, or grouped on the Select submenu of the Object menu. Here you can choose the object which is above or below the current object, which is contained in or the container or the current object, or which is the previous or next object in a group. These commands are also available on the context menu, and as buttons in the Control palette.

Locking

Many XPress users don't realize how fragile the Lock feature is in that program: While locked objects cannot be dragged with the Item tool, you can still change their position with the Measurement palette, the Modify dialog box or even by pressing the arrow keys on the keyboard. InDesign's implementation of the Lock feature works the way it does in PageMaker. To lock an object, select Lock Position from the Object menu or the context menu. When locked, an object can't be dragged, and can't be manipulated with the Transform palette or the transform tools. However, you can still change formatting attributes or edit text in a locked object. To unlock an object, select Unlock Position from the Object menu or context menu.

Another, even more powerful way of locking and unlocking is by organizing page objects on layers, and then locking layers (see Chapter 13).

12

Duplicating, Deleting, and Aligning Objects

Making copies of things and getting rid of them: What could be easier? Yet, there's more to this topic than meets the eye. In this short chapter we'll show you some methods which aren't in the QuarkXPress or PageMaker vocabulary.

Duplicating Objects

InDesign gives us several ways to duplicate objects—copying and pasting, Paste in Place, Duplicate, Step and Repeat, and Option/Alt-Dragging.

Copying and Pasting

You can cut, copy, and paste objects in InDesign with the Selection, Direct Selection and Type tools. When choosing Paste from the Edit menu (or pressing Command-V/Ctrl-V), InDesign pastes the object in the center of the current page or spread. You may need to be careful about which page the object is copied to. InDesign places the object on the *targeted* spread—the one whose number is highlighted in the Pages palette and displayed in the lower-left corner of the document window—not necessarily the page that is visible on screen.

If you select a graphic (the content) in a graphics frame with the Direct Selection tool and copy it, pasting with either the Selection or Direct Selection tool automatically creates a new frame in the middle of the page or spread. This can drive XPress users mad because if they select another frame and choose Paste, they expect the graphic to be pasted into it. Not so in InDesign. Here, you must choose Paste Into (Command-Option-V/Ctrl-Alt-V) if you want the graphic to end up inside a selected frame.

If you select some text from a text frame with the Type tool and copy it, what happens when you paste depends on the tool you have selected. As you'd expect, if you have an insertion point in a text frame, the text is pasted there. However, if you have the Selection or Direct Selection tool selected (there is no text insertion point), InDesign creates a new text frame in the center of the targeted page or spread and pastes the text into it.

Finally, if you select a *part* of a path (one or more segments or points) with the Direct Selection tool and copy it to the Clipboard, pasting creates a duplicate of the partial path (including any fill or stroke attributes) in the center of the current page or spread.

Paste in Place

InDesign also offers an extra Paste command, already familiar to Page-Maker users: Paste in Place. This is handy when you want to copy objects to other pages. Choose the objects you want to duplicate, and copy as usual. Then jump to the page or spread where you want the copy and choose Paste in Place from the Edit menu (or press Command-Option-Shift-V/Ctrl-Alt-Shift-V). The objects are pasted in the same X/Y position on the spread. The only thing tricky about this command is that if you're using facing pages, it always copies to the same page on the spread. That is, you can't copy from a left-hand page and then paste in place on a right-hand page; the object will end up on the left-hand page.

Duplicating and Step-and-Repeating

InDesign's Duplicate and Step and Repeat commands (in the Edit menu) are almost exactly like the features of the same name in XPress, though the default keyboard shortcuts are different: Command-Option-Shift-D/Ctrl-Alt-Shift-D duplicates any selected object down and to the right of the original object. To duplicate with precise offsets, press Command-

Figure 12-1
Step and Repeat
dialog box

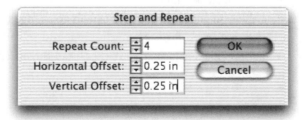

Shift-V/Ctrl-Shift-V) to open the Step and Repeat dialog box (see Figure 12-1). This feature lets you set the number of copies and the horizontal and vertical offset. Note that Duplicate does not use the last-used Step and Repeat offsets, like XPress's feature does.

Option/Alt-Dragging

Another method of duplicating is a feature borrowed from Illustrator and Photoshop, and involves holding down the Option/Alt key. Whenever you want to make a copy of something, you can hold down the Option/Alt key and drag with the Selection or Direct Selection tool to make a duplicate. If you have some other tool selected, then Command-Option/Ctrl-Alt-drag. A double-arrow cursor appears when dragging, indicating the duplication. Be sure to release the mouse button before releasing the Option/Alt key.

Deleting Objects

InDesign matches QuarkXPress's and PageMaker's two methods of deleting page objects: the Clear command (from the Edit menu, or press Delete) and the Cut command.

Aligning Objects

InDesign offers the very same abilities to align and distribute objects offered in QuarkXPress's Space/Align dialog box, using the Align palette, but we find its design is a great deal more intuitive.

To align or distribute objects, open the Align palette by choosing Align from the Window menu (or press F8), then show all its features by choosing Show Options from the palette menu. The Align palette is broken into five sections (see Figure 12-2). Remember that if you pause your cursor over a button, a tool tip provides a descriptive label.

Simple aligning is when you want two or more objects to align precisely along their sides or centers. In InDesign, you just click on one of the six icons in the top row of the palette—there are three for horizontal and three for vertical alignment.

InDesign aligns along the most-obvious edge (top-most for top-aligning, bottom-most for bottom-aligning, and so on). The one exception is when one object is locked; in that case, all the other objects move and the locked item stays put.

Building Pages

Figure 12-2
The Align palette

Horizontal Align options

Vertical Distribute Objects options

Distribute Objects Precisely option

Distribute Spacing Precisely option

Vertical Align options

Horizontal Distribute Objects options

Distribute Spacing options

Distributing Objects

Distributing objects (placing equal space between them) requires that you first select three or more objects.

Maintaining the Bounding Box

To distribute while maintaining the bounding box means the left-most and right-most (or top-most and bottom-most) objects stay put while the other objects move. You can do this by choosing one of the six icons in the second row, labeled Distribute Objects. For this to work, make sure the Use Spacing checkbox just below these icons is turned off.

Alternatively, you can move the objects so that the space between them is equal (this is what we use most often) by choosing one of the two buttons marked Distribute Spacing—one for Horizontal and one for Vertical. Again, make sure the Using Spacing checkbox is turned off.

Distributing Using Precise Spacing

There are two more kinds of object distribution which don't maintain the bounding box of the selected objects. Here you're attempting to place a precise amount of space between selected objects. To do this, turn on the Using Spacing option and enter a value in the Use Spacing field. The top-most or left-most object remains stationary, and the remaining objects space themselves in relation to that object. InDesign allows either positive or negative measurements; positive numbers move objects to the right or down, negative numbers to the left or up.

The last method of distribution specifies the spacing between object bounding boxes. You can do this by turning on the Using Spacing option at the bottom of the palette and choosing one of the two Distribute Spacing buttons.

13

Layers

You may be familiar with using layers in PageMaker, QuarkXPress 5 or 6, Illustrator, Freehand, or Photoshop. Artwork can be placed on different layers, and the layers can be shown or hidden, locked or unlocked, rearranged in the stacking order, and so on. Layers are particularly useful when creating multiple versions of a layout, or when you want to isolate elements like graphics and text in a complex layout.

It's important to realize that InDesign's layers are document-wide, so changing a layer applies to all the pages in your document.

InDesign, like other applications, controls layers with a Layers palette (see Figure 13-1). The palettes in each application look and work in many similar ways, but there are important differences as well; InDesign, like PageMaker, puts many of its controls on a palette flyout menu.

Basic Layer Operations

You can create a generic new layer (without naming it) by clicking the New Layer button on the Layers palette. InDesign automatically assigns a color and selects the layer so that objects you draw or place will be assigned to it. To create a layer and set its attributes (like its name) at the same time, either choose New Layer from the palette menu, or hold down the Option/Alt key while clicking the New Layer button. The Layer Options dialog box (see Figure 13-2) appears. You can also open this dialog box by double-clicking on any layer in the palette.

Building Pages

Figure 13-1
The Layers palette

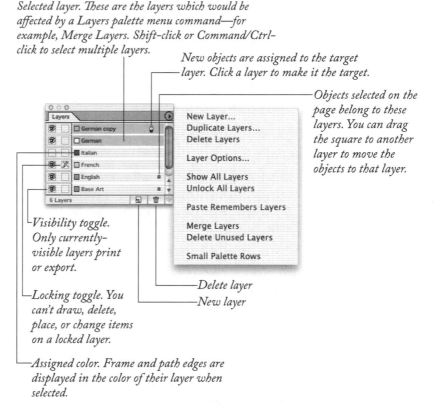

Selected layer. These are the layers which would be affected by a Layers palette menu command—for example, Merge Layers. Shift-click or Command/Ctrl-click to select multiple layers.

New objects are assigned to the target layer. Click a layer to make it the target.

Objects selected on the page belong to these layers. You can drag the square to another layer to move the objects to that layer.

Visibility toggle. Only currently-visible layers print or export.

Locking toggle. You can't draw, delete, place, or change items on a locked layer.

Assigned color. Frame and path edges are displayed in the color of their layer when selected.

Delete layer
New layer

Assigning Objects to Layers

Whenever you create a new object on your page, InDesign assigns it to the layer which has the pen icon on the Layers palette—called the *target layer*. To make a layer the target, just click on the layer's name.

If you want to move an object to a different layer, first select the object. (Note that Option/Alt-clicking the layer name selects all the objects on a layer.) You'll see a small square appear beside the name of the layer (or layers) the objects are on. Drag this square to the layer where you want to move the objects. The color of the objects' frame and selection handles will change to the new layer color. You can also duplicate the selected objects to another layer by holding down the Option/Alt key while dragging the square icon. Secret tip: If you want to drag to a locked or hidden layer, hold down the Command/Ctrl key when dragging.

Rearranging and Combining Layers

The order in which you see the layers in the Layers palette indicates their stacking order in the document. A layer at the top of the palette is "higher"

Figure 13-2

The Layer Options
dialog box

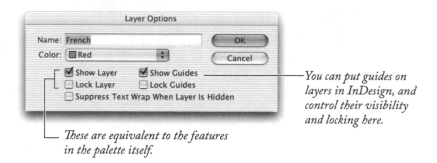

You can put guides on layers in InDesign, and control their visibility and locking here.

These are equivalent to the features in the palette itself.

in the stacking order than the layers below it, so its objects will obscure objects that are on layers "below" it. (The stacking commands discussed in Chapter 11 only apply to the stacking order *within a layer*.)

To rearrange the stacking order of layers, simply drag the layer up or down within the palette.

You can also combine the elements of two or more layers onto one: In the Layers palette, select the layers which you want to combine by Shift- or Command/Ctrl-clicking their names. Then choose Merge Layers from the palette menu.

Duplicating and Deleting Layers

Duplicating a layer makes a copy of the layer and all of the objects on it. You can do this by selecting the layer and choosing Duplicate Layer in the palette menu. Or, bypass the Layer Options dialog box by simply dragging the layer on top of the palette's New Layer button.

When you delete a layer in XPress, the program gives you the option of moving objects on that layer to another layer. You have no such luck in InDesign, which simply deletes all the objects on that layer. To delete a layer, select it and click the Delete Layer button (or choose Delete Layer from the palette menu). If you have a bunch of layers you're no longer using (there are no objects on them), you can select the Delete Unused Layers command on the palette menu to delete them.

PART 4

Building Documents

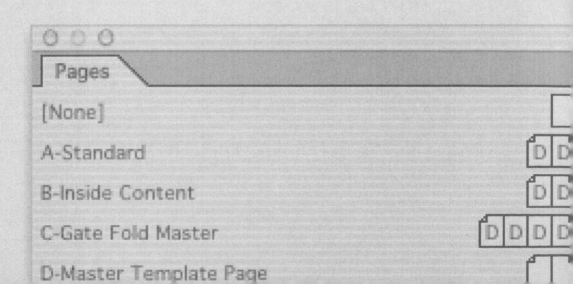

14

Creating, Opening, and Saving Documents

Creating new documents is one of InDesign's most straight-forward procedures. In the New Document dialog box (see Figure 14-1), you can define your document's specifications, including orientation (portrait or landscape), page size (from ⅙-inch per side to a maximum size of 18-feet per side), size of margins, and number of columns. The Master Text Frame feature is just like the Automatic Text Box checkbox in XPress: It creates a text frame within the margins of the master page. InDesign also lets you enter a number of pages (XPress doesn't let you do this, but PageMaker does). Your documents can be up to 9,999 pages long, for those of you who are counting.

Then, you can click the More Options button to set the following values:

- **Bleed.** This defines the distance outside the page area that is used for objects that print all of the way to the edge of a document. Bleed guides are automatically created around the perimeter of your page when you enter these values.

- **Slug.** To specify an area outside of the printed document where specific printing and production information is placed, such as a job number, you can enter a Slug value. As with Bleed values, guides are automatically created around the perimeter of your page when you enter these values.

Figure 14-1

The New Document
dialog box
(Click More Options
to see the options for
defining the Bleed
and Slug values for
your document.)

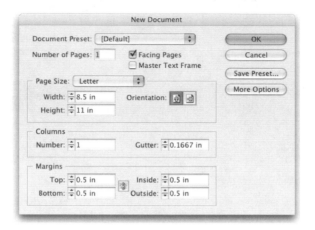

Once you set up the New Document dialog box just the way you want
it, consider clicking Save Preset so that you can get back to the same values
in the future.

You can also bypass the entire New Document dialog box by typing
Command-Option-N/Ctrl-Alt-N. In this case, InDesign creates a document using the last-used document preset you chose.

Default Page Sizes

You can easily customize the default page size by closing any InDesign
documents and choosing File, Document Setup. Use the Document Setup
window to enter the default page size, bleed, slug and number of pages.
The next time you go to create a new document, the values you entered in
the Document Setup window will be used. Similarly, when no documents
are open, you can choose Margins and Columns from the Margins menu
and set the default Margin and Column values.

Changing Page Size and Orientation

You're not stuck with a page size and orientation after you create a document. To change these, select Document Setup from the File menu. Here
you can change the number of pages, the page size and orientation, and
whether you're using facing pages.

Margin and column guides can also be changed, by choosing Margins
and Columns from the Layout menu. (In XPress, you can only change
these while on a master page, but InDesign lets you change them for
individual document pages, too.)

Opening Files

To open an InDesign file, choose Open from the File menu, double-click on the file on the desktop, or drag the file's icon onto the application icon. You can also open QuarkXPress and PageMaker documents with InDesign (see Appendix A and B). When opening InDesign files you can select from three options in the Open dialog box (see Figure 14-2).

- **Open Normal.** This is the default option and the one you'll use when you just want to edit an existing file. If you open a file saved as a template (see below), this option opens a new, Untitled document based on the template.

- **Open Original.** Use this option to open and edit a template file itself, instead of opening an Untitled file based on the template.

- **Open Copy.** With this option you can use any document as a starting point for a new document. To achieve the same result in QuarkXPress, you'd need to manually duplicate a document and then open it.

Figure 14-2
The Open dialog box

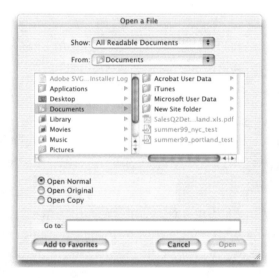

Saving Files

Use the Save As dialog box to specify whether a InDesign should save your file as a document or template. This choice has the same effect as choosing Document or Template in the Save As dialog box in QuarkXPress. The default, InDesign CS Document, saves a normal InDesign file; choose the InDesign CS Template option to be able to create new, untitled InDesign documents that use the current file's settings and contents.

Building Documents

15

Adding, Deleting, and Arranging Pages

The Pages palette provides control for managing pages in your InDesign documents. You can access the Pages palette from the Window menu (or press F12). By default, it displays master pages in the top section of the palette and document pages in the bottom (see Figure 15-1).

InDesign lets you customize the way the pages are displayed in the Pages palette: Select Palette Options from the Pages palette menu (see Figure 15-2). For example, we usually turn off the Show Vertically checkbox in the Pages section; it makes the palette look less like QuarkXPress, but it's a much better use of screen real estate.

Adding Pages to your Documents

You can add a single page by dragging one of the page icons from the master page section of the Pages palette to the document page section of the palette. Or, you can add a spread by dragging the master page name down instead of an icon.

In addition, you can use the New button at the bottom of the Pages palette to add a page to a document (the page is added at the end of the document). Or, hold down the Option/Alt key while clicking the New button to open the Insert Pages dialog box—letting you add multiple pages, and specify what master page they should be based on and where they should appear (see Figure 15-3). You can also get to this dialog box by choosing Insert Pages from the flyout menu of the Pages palette.

Figure 15-1
The Pages palette

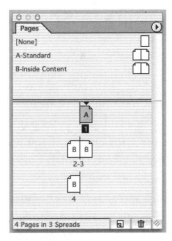

Figure 15-2
The Pages palette
Options dialog box

Arranging Pages

The InDesign Pages palette allows you to re-arrange pages by dragging page icons. As you are dragging a page icon within the palette, a thin vertical line appears in the location where the page will move if you drag the page between two spreads or between individual pages in a non-facing pages document. You can also move a page between two pages in an existing spread. Drag the page to be moved so that it is placed between the pages in a spread. An arrow appears showing the direction in which the spread pages will be relocated.

Deleting Pages

You can select a page or group of pages to be deleted and click the Delete icon at the bottom of the palette. Select more than one page with Command/Ctrl for non-contiguous pages, or use the Shift key for contiguous page ranges.

Creating a Multipage Spread

InDesign can create spreads that span more than two adjoining pages, which are sometimes referred to as gatefolds because they open similar to a gate. It's important to note that stand-alone gatefold documents, such as direct mail pieces with multiple folds, require a separate size for each fold so that inner pages fit inside the outer pages. InDesign requires all document pages to be the same size, so if you need these kinds of documents you should probably create them as one-page-per side and place fold marks where appropriate.

First, determine which spread is to be expanded beyond two pages, and then select that page (for single-sided documents) or spread (for facing pages documents) and choose Keep Spread Together from the palette menu in the Pages palette. The spread will then have brackets surrounding the page numbers (see Figure 15-3). You can then drag additional pages into the spread by dragging a master page icon next to the spread or dragging another page icon next to the spread.

Creating a Multipage Master Page

You can create a master page for gatefolds. This is sometimes the easiest way to build a gatefold. Select New Master from the flyout menu in the Pages palette. Enter the number of pages to be in the multipage spread and click OK. Use this master page to create as many gatefold pages as you need. This lets you bypass the process of selecting the Keep Spread Together option and then manually dragging pages into the gatefold.

Figure 15-3
Multipage spreads
are displayed with
brackets surrounding
their numbers.

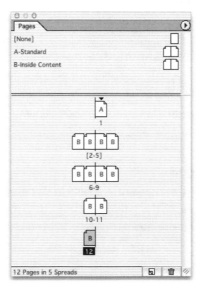

Targeting versus Selecting Pages

InDesign makes a distinction between *targeting* a page or spread and *selecting* a page or spread:

- A page (or spread) is *targeted* if it is the page onto which the next new objects will be placed, such as objects pasted into a document.

- A page (or spread) is *selected* if the next page action—like duplicating the spread—will affect that page or spread. The target page and the selected page can be different pages.

You may wonder why this distinction is useful: if you're looking at your document at a lower magnification (a birds-eye view, showing more than one page at a time), you may still want to place an object onto a certain page or spread. By targeting a spread, you can be certain as to where objects will be placed.

Targeting a Page or Spread

By default, the target spread is the spread that's centered in the document window, but you may want another spread to be targeted. Before performing an action that depends on the targeted spread, double-check which page or spread is actually targeted by finding the highlighted page numbers in the Pages palette—note that the page numbers can be highlighted without the page icons being highlighted. Target a page by clicking on any element on a page or clicking on the page or pasteboard within the document window. You can also target a spread by double-clicking the page numbers under the spread's page icons in the Pages palette (this centers that spread in the window).

Selecting a Page or Spread

You can select pages or spreads in the Pages palette to identify which pages will be affected by page-editing commands. Clicking once on a page icon in the Pages palette selects a page. Once a page or spread is selected you can use a command such as Margins and Columns on the Layout menu to edit the margins and number of columns on the selected page or spread.

You can select multiple pages or spreads by holding down the Shift key while selecting contiguous pages, or by holding down the Command/Ctrl key if they are discontiguous. Double-clicking on the page number beneath a page or spread will both target and select the page or spread.

16

Creating and Applying Master Pages

As with QuarkXPress and PageMaker, you can create master pages with InDesign to eliminate the need for repetitive page formatting. InDesign also includes additional master page features like parent-child ("based on") master pages and selective overriding of master page items.

Creating a New Master Page

To make a master page, select New Master from the Pages palette menu—or, faster, by Command-Option/Ctrl-Alt-clicking the new page button in the Pages palette. In the New Master dialog box (see Figure 16-1) you can then enter the number of pages in the master and identify if it is based upon another master page. We discuss these capabilities later in this chapter.

Automatic Linked Text Frames

On a single-sided master page, you don't have to do anything special to make a text frame "automatically" link from one page to the next. To make auto-linking text frames on a facing-pages master page, link the frame on the left page to the frame on the right page. We cover linking text frames in more detail in Chapter 20.

Unlike other programs, you can have more than one automatically-linked text frame per page. For instance, if you have two text frames per

Figure 16-1
The New Master
dialog box

master page, you can link the first on the left page to the first on the right page, and the second on the left page to the second on the right page.

Duplicating a Master Page

If you want to create a master page that is very similar to an existing master, you can duplicate a master page by choosing the master page to be duplicated and then choosing the Duplicate Spread command from the Pages palette's flyout menu. However, creating a "based on" relationship is even more powerful; we discuss that below.

Converting a Document Page into a Master Page

InDesign lets you turn a document page into a master page: Simply drag the document spread icon in the Pages palette to the master section of the Pages palette. If the original document spread was based upon a master page, changes to that master page will still impact both the document page and also the new master page that was built from the document page.

Creating Parent/Child Relationships

You can base one master page on another master page using a parent-child relationship. For example, many books and catalogs use several different, but very similar, master pages. By creating one "parent" master page and then basing the other "child" master pages on it, you can later make changes to the parent that ripple through to all the child master pages.

Making Child Masters

After building your parent master page, which contains all of the necessary elements to be shared with the child master pages, select the New Master command from the Pages palette menu (or Command-Option-click/Ctrl-Alt-click on the New Page button). In the New Master dialog box, choose the parent master page from the Based On popup menu. When you click OK, the new master page will be a child master page that is based on the parent master page (see Figure 16-2).

Building Documents

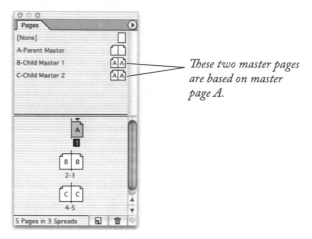

Figure 16-2

A master page can
be based on another
master page.

*These two master pages
are based on master
page A.*

You can also drag one master page icon on top of any other master page in the Pages palette. The page you drag becomes a parent master, the page you drop it on becomes a child master. The prefix on the master page icon indicates the relationship.

Applying Master Pages to Document Pages

To apply a master page to a document page you can drag the master page on top of a document page icon or the page numbers below the icons in the Pages palette. Additionally, you can select one or more document pages (remember you can Command/Ctrl-click to select discontiguous pages) and then Option/Alt-click on the master page you want to apply.

There's one other way to apply a master page to one or more document pages: Select Apply Master to Pages from the Pages palette menu. InDesign lets you select a master to apply and a page range. For instance, you could apply B-Master to pages "2, 4-5, 11-16, 22".

Just as in QuarkXPress, each document page icon in the Pages palette is marked with the prefix of the master page applied to it.

Changing Master Items

In PageMaker, you can't edit master page items on master pages. In Quark-XPress, it's too easy to edit them. InDesign strikes a balance. If you need to modify a master item on a document page you must Command-Shift-click/Ctrl-Shift-click on it with any tool. This also works to select parent items on a child master page. After selecting a master page item, it then becomes a part of the local document page. This is called *overriding* the master page item. You can override all master page items by choosing Override All Master Page Items from the Pages palette menu.

When you override a master page item, you can make local changes to it. For example, you can override a master frame and then change the thickness of the stroke around the frame. However, changing the stroke thickness only overrides this one attribute; the fill color and other attributes are still linked back to the master page item. If you change the fill color on the master page, it *does* update on the document page, even though the object has been overridden. If you don't want any link between an object and its original master page, first override it and then (while it's selected) choose Detach Selection From Master from the Pages palette menu. *Detaching* means there's no longer a link to the master page item.

Note that the act of overriding an object always breaks the link to a frame's content. That is, even if you just override a text or graphic frame and then don't actually change anything else about it, the content (the text or the picture inside the frame) is no longer linked to the master page.

You don't actually need to select master page items when placing imported text or graphics. InDesign is smart enough to know that if you click a loaded Place icon on a master page frame, the master frame should accept the content. That means that you only need to override a master page item when you need to change something about the object.

Removing Master Item Changes

InDesign can remove changes you've made to specific master items. You can remove changes to individual items or to all master items that have been modified on a spread.

To eliminate changes to a specific master item, select the item and choose Remove Selected Local Overrides from the Pages palette's flyout menu. Or, if you want all the overridden master page items on a spread to revert back to their original state, first deselect all objects and then choose Remove All Local Overrides from the flyout menu. This only works for objects that have local overrides, *not* for objects that have been detached from the master page.

Building Documents

17

Grids and Guides

At first glance, InDesign's ruler guides work in much the same way they do in many other programs. You can simply pull a guide from the vertical or horizontal ruler and drag it onto the page. Ruler guides that are dragged and released over the page appear only on the page, while guides released with the mouse over the pasteboard extend over both the page and the pasteboard—across all pages in a spread.

However, InDesign's ruler guides act just like page elements, so you can select one or more guides at a time, copy and paste them, and even position selected guides numerically using the Control or Transform palettes. Guides, like any other object, can be placed on a layer. As with all other objects, a guide belongs to the layer that was active when you create it.

Customizing Ruler Guides

Using the Ruler Guides feature from the Layout menu (see Figure 17-1) you can choose these options:

- **View Threshold.** Determines the magnification above which a guide is displayed and below which a guide is hidden. This is equivalent to when you Shift-drag as you create a guide in QuarkXPress.

- **Color.** A guide is displayed using this color when it isn't selected. When you select a guide, it appears in its layer's color.

Because InDesign works with guides as objects, you can change the settings for one or more guides simultaneously by selecting the guides before choosing the Ruler Guides command. Or, to change the default settings for future guides, choose the Ruler Guides command when no guides are selected. You can also access this feature with the context menu (Control- or right-clicking on a guide).

Figure 17-1
The Ruler Guides
dialog box

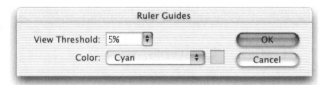

Treating guides as objects takes some getting used to, but there are great benefits. For example, you can use the arrow keys to nudge one or more selected guides slightly. If you need to create more than one guide, you might want to place one on the page and then use the Step and Repeat command (on the Edit menu) to repeat it at regular intervals. (You can also use the Create Guides command described on the next page.)

Here are a few other guide tricks.

- To convert a page guide into a pasteboard guide (one that extends across a spread and onto the pasteboard), hold down the Command/Ctrl key while you drag it.

- If you know where you want a pasteboard guide, you can place one quickly by double-clicking in the ruler at that point. For example, if you want a horizontal guide at 4 inches, double-click at the 4-inch mark on the vertical ruler. Even better, hold down the Shift key when you double-click and InDesign will snap the guide to the nearest ruler tick, so you don't have to worry if your cursor is positioned exactly where you want the guide.

- You can place a horizontal and a vertical guide at the same time by Command/Ctrl-dragging from the intersection of the two rulers. Or, better, Command-Shift/Ctrl-Shift-drag to snap the guides to the nearest ruler ticks.

- When you copy and paste one or more guides, InDesign always remembers the guide's position on the page.

Locking Guides

Note that guides, like any object, can be locked in place by selecting Lock Position from the Object menu. You can also lock all the guides in the document at once with the Lock Guides feature in the View menu. Finally, you can lock one or more guides by placing them on a locked layer.

Deleting Guides

To delete a guide, just select it and press the Delete key on your keyboard. This is very different than the "drag out of the window" method that XPress uses. You can delete all the guides on a spread at once with—ironically—the Create Guides feature (below).

Create Guides

The Create Guides feature (in the Layout menu) allows you to expand beyond the options of the Margins and Columns command. The Create Guides dialog box (see Figure 17-2) includes these options:

- **Number.** Sets the number of rows or columns you want to create using guides.

- **Gutter.** If the Gutter setting is larger than zero, InDesign places two guides in each location, rather than one; the amount of space between the two guides equals the Gutter value. If you want four evenly-spaced guides on your page, set the Number to 5 (one more than the number of guides) and the Gutter to zero.

- **Fit Guides To.** Adjusts the row and column spacing based on the page edges or margins.

- **Remove Existing Ruler Guides.** Clears all page guides, useful when you want to remove guides you were using to roughly sketch out the layout.

Working with Margin Guides

The margin and column guides on each document page reflect those on the master page. However, you can override the margin and column guides on individual document pages.

By default, the margin guides are pink (magenta) and the column guides are violet. That's why in a normal, one-column document the top and bottom margins appear pink and the left and right margins appear purple—because the column guides are overlapping the margin guides. If you wish, you can change the guide colors in the Guides panel of the Preferences dialog box.

Hiding Guides

To turn off the display of guides, choose Hide Guides from the View menu (or press Command-;/Ctrl-;). Hiding a layer also hides all guides

Figure 17-2
The Create Guides dialog box makes it easy to add more column and row variations to your InDesign layouts.

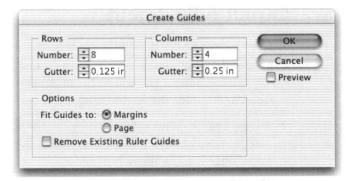

on that layer. You can also turn on the Preview mode in the Tools palette (or press W when not editing text) to hide all non-printing objects, including guides.

Editing Margin & Column Guides

Before you edit your margin or column guides, select the pages or pages you wish to modify in the Pages palette. Next, choose Margin and Columns from the Layout menu and enter the desired values in the Margins and Columns dialog box (see Figure 17-3). We like to turn on the Preview checkbox so we can see the effect before clicking OK. Whether or not the objects on your page change (like text frames resizing to the new margins) after you click OK depends on the Layout Adjustment option (see the next page).

Figure 17-3
The Margins and Columns dialog box

As with other attributes, changing the values in the Margins and Columns dialog box while no documents are open establishes a new, default set of values for all future documents you create.

Editing columns with the Margin and Columns dialog box always results in equally-sized columns. If you need unequal columns—like a larger column on the left—you can drag the column guides on the page to the location where you want them.

Building Documents

Layout Adjustment

If you enable the Layout Adjustment feature, found in the Layout menu (see Figure 17-4), any box that reaches to the margin guides automatically resizes when you make changes to the margin guide values.

You can fine-tune the feature using these options:

- **Enable Layout Adjustment.** Lets layout adjustment happen. It's important to note that when this is on, layout adjustment occurs whenever you change margin or column guides.

- **Snap Zone.** If an object is closer than this distance to a guide, it's considered aligned to that guide and may be moved or resized during layout adjustment.

- **Allow Graphics and Groups to Resize.** Enables graphics and groups to be scaled during a layout adjustment. Text frames are always scaled if needed.

- **Allow Ruler Guides to Move.** You might leave this on if you want ruler guides to be proportionally repositioned relative to the new margin or column settings.

- **Ignore Ruler Guide Alignments.** When this is on, objects won't be adjusted to stay aligned to ruler guide position changes.

- **Ignore Object and Layer Locks.** When this is on, locked objects are allowed to move to follow changes to guide positions.

Use layout adjustment with care. It can save you tons of time when repurposing content for radically different page sizes or layouts. But it does not work with every layout and you can end up with a disastrous mess. If that's the case, remember InDesign's multiple undo! It works best when your layout was designed from the start with resizing and repositioning in mind, such as keeping all objects clearly aligned to column guides and margins and leaving space for adjustments. Note that layout adjustment applies to all pages, not just the page you're looking at.

Figure 17-4
The Layout
Adjustment
dialog box

Baseline Grid

The baseline grid is used to align the baseline of text across multiple columns on a page or spread. Alignment is a paragraph attribute, and you can force text to align to the baseline grid in by clicking the Lock to Baseline Grid button in the Paragraph or Control palette.

The starting point of the baseline grid, how frequently it is repeated and at what view percentage it become visible or hidden are defined by settings in the Grids panel of the Preferences dialog box.

You can make the baseline grid visible or invisible by selecting Show/Hide Baseline Grid from the View menu (or press Command-Option-'/Ctrl-Alt-'). The Show/Hide Baseline Grid command is also available in the context-sensitive menu when clicking an empty area of the document.

Here's a hidden trick: InDesign lets you lock the *first line* of a paragraph to the baseline grid, leaving alone the rest of the paragraph's spacing. To do this, first turn on the Lock to Baseline Grid feature for the paragraph. Then choose Only Align First Line to Grid from the flyout menu in the Control or the Paragraph palette.

Document Grid

The document grid supplements margin and column guides and creates a grid across the entire document—like an enormous piece of graph paper. The grid makes it possible to align elements vertically and horizontally without having to build individual ruler guides.

You can define the starting point and increments of the document grid in the Grids panel of the Preferences dialog box. This also lets you set the grid color, the measure between each horizontal and vertical gridline, and the subdivisions between the gridlines.

Then, to make the document grid visible or invisible, select Show/Hide Document Grid from the View menu (or press Command-'/Ctrl-'). You can turn on and off whether objects snap to the grid by selecting or unselecting Snap to Document Grid from the View menu (or press Command-Shift-'/Ctrl-Shift-').

18

Numbering and Sectioning

InDesign lets you create multiple sections within a document. For example, the numbering scheme of a book's front matter, table of contents and index may be different from that of its body. Perhaps you'll use roman numerals for the preface and regular ("Arabic") numerals for the body of the book. You can control your document's sections using the Pages palette.

Creating Sections

To create a section, select the page where you want the section to start in the Pages palette, then choose Numbering & Section Options from the palette menu. In the New Section dialog box (see Figure 18-1), turn on the Start Section checkbox to start a new section on the selected page.

Section Options

If you want the section to begin with a specific page number, choose Start Page Numbering At and type the page number. Otherwise, if the page numbering simply continues from the previous section, use the Automatic numbering option.

Prefixes

You can enter a Section Prefix if you would like the page numbers to be preceded by a label of 5 characters or fewer. For example, enter "A-" if you want the pages within this section to appear as *A-1, A-2,* and so on. By default, InDesign adds a Section Prefix of "Sec1:" to the first section, and so on. This is incredibly annoying, and most of the time we just delete that prefix or replace it with our own.

Style

The Style popup menu lets you determine whether the pages within a section are numbered using Arabic page numbering (which should be called "European" numbering, but don't get us started!), Roman numerals, or letters.

Section Marker

InDesign's Section Marker option lets you enter variable text that will be inserted whenever you use the Section Name command from the Insert Special Character menu. For example, see the header at the top of this page (the one that has the chapter number and title)? That was created with a single Section Marker character in a text frame on the master page. Then, for each chapter in this book, we started a new section and typed that number and title into the Section Marker field.

On each document page, the special character is replaced automatically with the proper section information. This is much faster than creating a different master page for each chapter.

Figure 18-1
Numbering and
Section Options

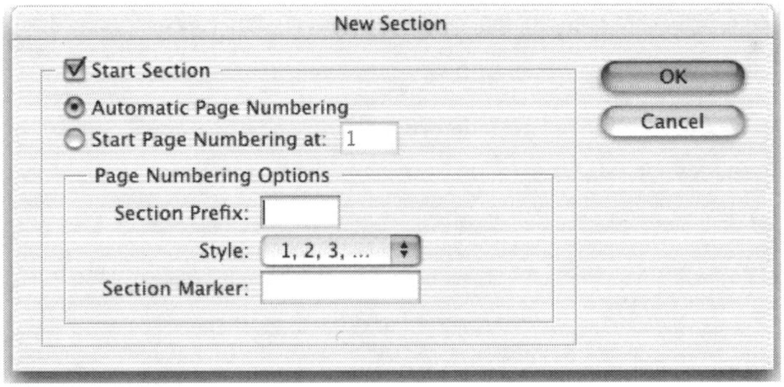

Editing Sections

When you create a section, InDesign places a black triangle above the page icon in the Pages palette. To change the section's settings, double-click the section triangle icon. If you need to delete a section, open the Numbering & Section Options dialog box for the first page of that section and turn off the Start Section option.

By the way, here's two tips if you're using many sections within a document. First, when you're specifying page numbers in the Print dialog box (or any other place you type a page number), InDesign expects you to type the page number just the way it appears on the page. If you want to type an absolute page number—based upon the page's position from the start of the document, like "the fifth page"—then type a plus sign before the number.

Also, you can have InDesign display the absolute page numbers rather than the section numbering by changing this option in the General Preferences dialog box. Absolute numbering displays all page numbers based on their position in the document, not the section number assigned to them. This affects only the displayed number for navigational purposes within InDesign, not the page numbers that print.

Typography

19

Importing and Editing Text

Most of the time, whether you're working with QuarkXPress, PageMaker, or InDesign, you import text from a Microsoft Word file (or some other word processor). However, sometimes we need to type text in the program, or do heavy amounts of editing in InDesign after text has already been placed. This chapter gives you some tips on how to do this easily in InDesign. We'll also tell you what your options are when importing text, and when flowing text through InDesign pages.

Selecting, Deleting, and Navigating

While text must always be placed in a text frame, remember that you can drag out a rectangular frame with the Type tool (press T). Once you have a frame, you can begin typing. In addition to the usual ability to select text by dragging the cursor, you can also use these shortcuts:

- Double-clicking selects a word.
- Triple-clicking selects a line.
- Quadruple-clicking selects a paragraph.
- Clicking five times (or pressing Command-A/Ctrl-A) selects all the text in your threaded text frames.

However, if you turn off the Triple Click to Select a Line option in the Text panel of the Preferences dialog box, then clicking three times selects a paragraph and four times selects the whole story.

If you have the Selection or Direct Selection tool selected, double-clicking a text frame switches to the Type tool and places an insertion point where you double-click. The Delete key strikes the character to the left of the cursor, and Shift-Delete removes the character to the right of the insertion point.

Keyboard Navigating

You can, of course, use the same keyboard shortcuts as PageMaker or QuarkXPress for navigating through your text, using the up, down, left and right arrow keys. Adding the Command/Ctrl key to the arrow keys moves by word or paragraph.

However, some shortcuts are different than XPress: The Home key takes you to the start of a line, and the End key to the end of the line. Command/Ctrl-Home takes you to the beginning of the story, and Command/Ctrl-End takes you to the end.

If you add the Shift key to each of these keyboard commands, InDesign selects all the text from the insertion point's location to the location where the command sends it.

Hidden Characters

InDesign calls characters that don't print—tabs, spaces, ends of paragraphs, and so on—*hidden characters*, and you make them visible (or invisible again) by selecting Show Hidden Characters from the Type menu or pressing Command-Option-I/Ctrl-Alt-I. Unlike PageMaker, these are visible in both layout and Story Editor views.

Story Editor

InDesign gives you two ways of viewing and editing a story: layout view (your normal document page), and the Story Editor view, a simple text-editor view which PageMaker users are familiar with. You can open a Story Editor window for any story by choosing Edit in Story Editor from the Edit menu, or pressing Command-Y/Ctrl-Y.

The Story Editor is particularly useful when you're working with type which is small or hard-to-read. You can type as fast as you want to in the Story Editor, and when you pause, InDesign updates the display of your story in layout view.

You can select preferences for how the Story Editor displays by choosing the Story Editor Display Preferences.

The Info Palette

Sometimes when you're typing or editing, you need to know how much text you have. You can tell this in InDesign by using the Info Palette (choose Info from the Window menu). When you click an insertion point in a story, it displays the number of characters, words, lines and paragraphs in the story. If you make it a selection, it shows you the same information for your selection.

Sometimes the Info palette displays the number of words like "465+30." That number after the plus sign is the number of overset words (words that can't fit in the text frame). You can see the whole story—including overset words—when you open the Story Editor.

Import Filters

InDesign can import text files from recent versions of Microsoft Word and Excel, files in Rich Text Format (RTF—a common interchange format), and tagged text format files.

As with PageMaker or QuarkXPress, for InDesign to be able to bring in data from another file format, it must have an import filter for that format. For text, word processing and RTF files, InDesign brings in most paragraph and character attributes and ignores most page layout information. It also imports paragraph and character styles if they're saved with the document. InDesign can also directly import tables from Microsoft Word documents and Excel spreadsheets from Office 97/98 and later versions (we discuss how to create tables in Chapter 35).

Import Options

When you choose the Place command, InDesign offers several import options (see Figure 19-1). There are two checkbox options which are always available:

- **Show Import Options.** This tells InDesign to display the Import Options dialog box (after you click the Open button or double-click on the file name), which offers different settings depending on the file format. Holding down the Shift key when you select a file does the same thing as turning on this checkbox.

- **Replace Selected Item.** When this is on, InDesign goes ahead and places the text (either at the current insertion point or replacing the text in any selected text frame); when off, the program displays the "Place gun" (which we describe in the next section).

Typography

Formatted or Unformatted Text

When you place a Microsoft Word or RTF file, it probably contains formatting applied in the word processing application. If you turn on the Remove Text and Table Formatting option in the Import Options dialog box, this formatting gets removed; if it is deselected, it will be retained.

Figure 19-1

The Place dialog box

Flowing Text

After making your import choices for one of the formats above, click Open. Then, one of two things happens: If you don't have a frame selected, you'll see the loaded text cursor (also called the "Place gun"), which changes depending on where the cursor is and what modifier keys you're holding down (see below).

If you have a frame (either text or graphics) selected and the Replace Selected Item option was turned on, InDesign fills the frame with the imported text. (If this was a mistake, just choose Undo Replace from the Edit menu, or press Command-Z/Ctrl-Z, which reloads the "Place gun," letting you place the text elsewhere.)

Manual Flow

You can manually flow text from one unlinked frame to the next by clicking the loaded text cursor anywhere on the page (see Figure 19-2). If you click on a frame, the text is placed into it. If you click elsewhere on the page, InDesign creates a frame and flows the text from the point where you click to the bottom of the page (or to the end of the text, whichever

Figure 19-2
Text flow cursors

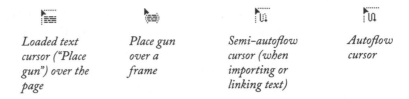

Loaded text cursor ("Place gun") over the page

Place gun over a frame

Semi-autoflow cursor (when importing or linking text)

Autoflow cursor

comes first). If there's more text than can fit in that frame (overset text), you'll see a plus sign in the out port of the text frame (we discuss the in and out ports in the next chapter). Instead of clicking, you can also drag out a text frame with the cursor to create the shape of a rectangular frame.

To continue manually flowing text, choose the Selection tool and click the frame's out port. This loads the text cursor, with which you can link the frame to another frame, or create a frame elsewhere in your document. Note that you can change pages or scroll around while the loaded text cursor is showing. (You can also cancel the Place gun by selecting any other tool in the Tools palette.)

Semi-Autoflow

Semi-autoflow works the same as manual text flow, except that after creating each text frame, the cursor automatically changes to the loaded text cursor ("reloads the gun") so you can create another text frame or fill an existing frame without manually clicking on the out port. You can choose the semi-autoflow method by holding down the Option/Alt key when placing text. InDesign then displays the semi-autoflow cursor.

Autoflow

If you hold down the Shift key when you click with the loaded text cursor, InDesign flows your text automatically, creating new frames and pages, and linking them automatically (this is the default behavior of XPress). If you Shift-click on a frame from a master page, InDesign automatically adds new document pages and links from one master page text frame to the next. Unfortunately, unlike QuarkXPress, InDesign can't automatically add pages and text frames when editing text—only when importing with the Shift key.

Linking to Text Files

If you turn on Create Links When Placing Text and Spreadsheet Files in the Text panel of the Preferences dialog box, InDesign maintains a link (in the Links palette) to the original file on disk. Then, if the original file is edited, InDesign alerts you that it has been modified. This is, of course, totally different than the way QuarkXPress and PageMaker works, but it can be useful in some workflows. Warning: If you update the modified text file, you will lose any editing or formatting that you performed in InDesign (it basically just re-imports the file).

Pasting Text

While placing is usually the preferred way to import text, you can also paste text from another InDesign document, or from some other application. When pasting text from another application, InDesign can retain the character and paragraph formatting attributes and any word processing styling, or it can strip all formatting for you. The choice depends on the Preserve Text Attributes When Pasting option in InDesign's General Preferences dialog box. If the option is turned on, formatting is preserved; if turned off, formatting is discarded. When copying from one InDesign file to another, formatting is always retained.

Creating Placeholder Text

InDesign makes it easy to create placeholder text when you're creating a preliminary layout: First, either place an insertion point in a text frame with the Type tool, or select one or more text frames with the Selection tool. Then choose Fill with Placeholder Text from the Type menu or the context menu. Dummy text fills the frames, and continues through any threaded frames.

If you don't like the "lorem ipsum" placeholder text InDesign uses, you can create your own by saving a text-only file with the name "placeholder.txt" in your InDesign application folder.

20

Threading and Unthreading Text Frames

What do you do when you have more text than can fit in one text frame? In this chapter, we'll explain *threading* and *unthreading* text frames, which works more similarly to PageMaker than to QuarkXPress.

When you select a text frame with the Selection tool, you can see an *in port* at the upper left corner of the frame, and an *out port* on the lower right corner (see Figure 20-1). The in port of the first box in a thread is always empty. A red plus sign in the out port of a frame means there's more text than can fit (the text is *overset*). When a triangle appears in an in or out port, it's an indicator that the text thread is continuing: In an in port, there is text coming *in* from another frame preceding this frame; in an out port, text continues *out* to another frame following this frame.

The threading of text frames is indicated by a text thread—a line in the color of the current layer which connects the frames. To see the thread, select any frame in the thread with the Selection or Direct Select tool and choose Show/Hide Text Threads from the View menu (or press Command-Option-Y/Ctrl-Alt-Y).

Threading

It's easy to link text frames together: With the Selection tool, select a frame and then click its out port. You'll see the loaded text cursor (see Figure 19-2). Then you may do one of the two following actions:

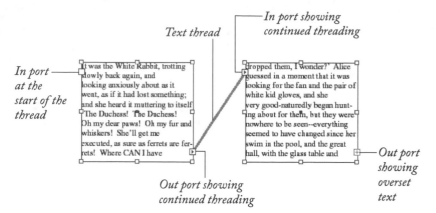

Figure 20-1
Threaded text frames

In port at the start of the thread

Text thread

In port showing continued threading

Out port showing continued threading

Out port showing overset text

- Drag out a new text frame. InDesign automatically links the current frame to this new frame.

- Click on another text frame to link the current frame to that one.

If there's a lot of overset text in the first frame, you may also hold down the Option/Alt key to use semi-autoflow or the Shift key to use autoflow, as we described in the previous chapter.

Unthreading

To disconnect two frames in the text chain—stopping the text flow at that point—use the Selection tool to select the frame before where you want to make the break and double-click its out port. Or, you can also select the subsequent frame and double-click on its in port.

Removing a Frame from the Chain

Finally, you may want to remove one or more frames from a text chain. If you want to delete the whole frame, select it and press the Delete key. The frame is deleted, but the text flows on into the succeeding frames in the chain. (Text is never removed from the chain when a frame is deleted.)

If you want to cut the frame and use it elsewhere, choose Cut from the Edit menu (or press Command-X/Ctrl-X). The text flows into the succeeding frames in the chain. Then go to the page where you the frame to appear, and choose Paste from the Edit menu, or press Command-V/Ctrl-V. The frame appears with the text which was in the previous location, but it is now disconnected from the chain. You can also Option/Alt-drag the text frame with the Selection tool to duplicate it (text and all).

21

Checking Spelling and Using Dictionaries

Whether you've imported text into your document or typed it directly, you'll probably want to check the spelling before you go to press. When InDesign checks spelling it highlights words which are misspelled or unknown, based on whatever language dictionaries you've assigned to your text (we discuss how to assign a language later in this chapter).

Picking a Search Range

InDesign can check the spelling of a word, a selection of text, your current story, or your current document. It can also search multiple selected stories and all of your stories in all open documents. It's not necessary to separately check your master pages, as you must do in XPress, since InDesign searches master pages whenever you search your document.

- To select a word or a range of text, just select it with the Type tool.

- To select a story, either click within the story with the Type tool, or select the story's frame with the Selection tool (or one frame from a series of linked frames). To select multiple stories, Shift-select their frames with the Selection tool.

- To search one or more documents, make sure they're open.

After making your selection, choose Check Spelling from the Edit menu (or press Command-I/Ctrl-I). InDesign displays the Check Spell-

Figure 21-1
Check Spelling
dialog box

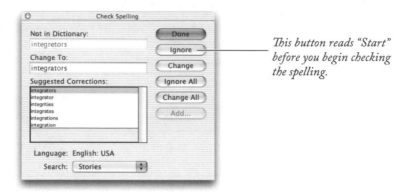

This button reads "Start" before you begin checking the spelling.

ing dialog box (see Figure 21-1). Select the range to be checked in the Search popup menu: Selection, Story, Stories, To End of Story, Document, or All Documents.

Performing a Search

When you're ready to begin the spell-checking process, click the Start button. As InDesign searches the text, it highlights each suspect word at the top of the dialog box and displays one of these messages: Not in Dictionary, Capitalization Error, Duplicate Word, or Unknown Word. Unlike XPress, InDesign shows replacement suggestions from its dictionary immediately.

- If you'd like InDesign to skip the word and not change anything, click either Ignore or Ignore All. Selecting Ignore skips the current instance of the word. Selecting Ignore All skips all instances of the word until you quit InDesign.

- If you'd like InDesign to replace the word, either type in the correct word in the Change To field or select a word in the Suggested Corrections list. Click Change to change that single instance of the word, or Change All to search the current range and change all instances. After a Change All command, InDesign displays a dialog box telling you how many replacements were made.

- If you'd like InDesign to add the word to your user-editable dictionary, click Add to open the Dictionary dialog box.

When InDesign has completed the search, it displays a Spell Check Complete message. If you want to stop the search before completion, just click the Done button.

Foreign Languages and Dictionaries

InDesign takes a very international point of view: Out of the box, it includes 20 dictionaries for 12 languages which are used for spell-checking and hyphenation. (However, to use languages beyond those included—like Japanese or Hebrew—you must purchase a special language edition of InDesign.) The extra dictionaries are installed by default.

Applying Language to Text

InDesign sees language as a character attribute. That means you can select any amount of text you want with the Type tool and choose a language in the Language popup menu on the Character or Control palette. You can also set a character or paragraph style to a specific language. (We discuss character formatting in Chapter 22 and we explore paragraph and character styles in Chapter 26.)

This means you can mix languages within the same paragraph, and when InDesign is either spell-checking or hyphenating, it uses the appropriate language dictionary for the text it is working with.

Adding or Removing Words

You can add or remove words from InDesign's user dictionary using the Dictionary dialog box (see Figure 21-2), which you can get to by selecting Dictionary from the Edit menu or by clicking the Add button in the Check Spelling dialog box. If you have a word selected in either your story or the Check Spelling dialog box, it automatically appears in the Word field—or you can just type one in. Then fill out the other settings in the Dictionary dialog box:

- Choose a language dictionary from the Language popup menu.

- When you add or remove words in a dictionary, InDesign actually adds the word to one of two lists: the Added Words exception list and the Removed Words exception list. For example, words added in the English (USA) language are stored in the ENG.UDC file. Select either Added Words or Removed Words from the Dictionary List popup menu.

- To change where the added or removed word is stored, use the Target popup menu. The default is the external user dictionary, but you can select any currently open document instead. The advantage of storing in the document is that this makes the change transportable. The

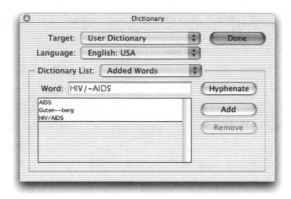

Figure 21-2

The Dictionary
dialog box

advantage of storing exceptions outside the document is that you can use them with multiple documents.

Finally, click the Add button to add the word to the exception list.

Hyphenation Points

You can examine InDesign's hyphenation break-points for a word, or change them if you like. In the Dictionary dialog box, when there is a word in the Word field, click Hyphenate to see that word's default hyphenation. InDesign's dictionaries rank syllable breaks for desirability. You can change these hyphenation points:

- Type one tilde (~) to indicate the best (or only) hyphenation point.

- Type two tildes (~~) for your second choice point.

- If necessary, type three tildes (~~~) for your last choice point.

- To prevent hyphenation, type a tilde before the first letter.

    When you're finished editing your added words, click Done.

Removing Words

To remove a word from one of the exceptions lists, choose Dictionary from the Edit menu. In the Target menu, choose the dictionary (external or document) from which you want to remove a word. Choose whether you want to modify the list of Added Words or Removed Words in the Dictionary List menu. In the word list, select the word and click Remove. When you're finished editing the lists, click Done.

22

Character Formatting

In this chapter, we begin to consider the kinds of formatting which can be applied to text, and how that is done in InDesign. This chapter focuses on character-level formatting, including selecting such things as typeface, font size, type styling attributes, and so on. One big difference between the programs: InDesign and PageMaker treat leading as a character attribute, rather than as a paragraph attribute, as XPress does. Fortunately, we'll tell you about a preference that can change that.

Selecting Text for Formatting

As with many other functions, InDesign gives you more flexibility than PageMaker and QuarkXPress in how you select text for formatting. Besides the obvious method of using the Type tool to select a range of text in a text frame, you can also:

- Use the Selection tool to select one or more unlinked text frames. Formatting applies to all the text in the selected frames. This can be a very quick way of selecting several small text frames—captions, for example—and formatting them all at the same time.

- In addition, character attributes can be copied with the Eyedropper tool and applied to other type. You can choose which attributes are copied. We discuss this in Chapter 38.

Basic Character Formatting

We'll start by considering the text attributes you probably change the most often: typeface, font size, and leading.

Typeface

InDesign lists fonts in the Character palette (see Figure 22-1), the Control palette and the Type menu. InDesign creates its own hierarchical font menus based on font family, so the order of your fonts in the list may be different than you expect.

If the Character palette isn't visible, you can choose Character from the Type menu. You can also press Command-T/Ctrl-T, which also activates the Font family field—or Command-6/Ctrl-6 which jumps to the first field in the Control palette. You type the first few characters of a typeface name and the menu jumps to the proper font. You can also choose a typeface by selecting it from the Font submenu in the Type menu.

Font Size

You can choose type size in the Character or Control palette or the Type menu. InDesign offers preset sizes and also lets you type your own. You can make text up to 1296 points (18 inches) large, and use the up and down arrow keys to adjust the size in 1-point increments. (Hold down the Shift key to change the size in 10-point increments.)

Leading

QuarkXPress users may wonder why InDesign considers leading a character attribute instead of a paragraph attribute. What's important is that you can set it the way you want. If you like the XPress way of doing it, turn on the Apply Leading to Entire Paragraphs option in the Text panel in the

Figure 22-1
The Character palette

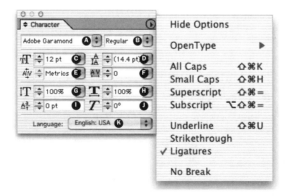

A *Font family*
B *Type style*
C *Font size*
D *Leading*
E *Kerning*
F *Tracking*
G *Vertical scale*
H *Horizontal scale*
I *Baseline shift*
J *Skew*
K *Language*

Preferences dialog box. Do this when no documents are open, and it will apply to all new documents you create.

In InDesign, you can set leading in the Character or Control palette, or with keystrokes. In the Character or Control palette, use similar methods to those described above: select a preset value, type your own value, or use the up/down arrows to change the leading value. Leading can be set in .001-point increments from 0 to 5000 points.

If you see a number in the Leading menu surrounded by parentheses, that's the current Auto leading value. To select Auto leading, choose Auto from the Leading popup menu on the palette. Auto leading is normally 120-percent of the font size of the largest character.

Kerning and Tracking

Kerning and tracking remove or add space between character pairs. *Kerning* adjusts spacing between two characters. *Tracking* changes the spacing for all character pairs in a range of text (PageMaker calls this *range kerning*). Kerning and tracking are measured in units relative to the size of the typeface—in *ems*. Note that by default XPress defines an em as the width of two zeros next to each other in a given font and size. InDesign uses a more standard value: An em equals the point size, so in 24-point text, one em is 24 points wide.

Metrics Kerning

Normally, if you select a range of text you'll see the word "Metrics" on the Kerning popup menu in the Character or Control palette. If you click an insertion point between two characters, the Kerning menu shows the value of the font kern pair in thousandths of an em: It will show a number like "0" (no kerning) or "(–70)" (which means that the current font has a kern pair that reduces the space by $^{70}\!/_{1,000}$ of an em). To apply Metrics kerning (removing any manual kerning), select a range of characters with the Type tool or one or more unlinked text frames with the Selection tool, then choose Metrics in the Kerning popup menu.

Manual Kerning

If you want to manually kern in InDesign, place the text insertion point between two characters. Then, in the Kerning field of the palette, either choose from the preset kerning values in the popup menu, type your own value, or use the up/down arrows to change the units of kerning (add Shift to increase/decrease in larger increments). You can also use keystrokes:

Hold down the Option/Alt key, and press the Left or Right Arrow keys to decrease or increase the space—by default in $^{20}/_{1,000}$ of an em.

Optical Kerning

If you choose Optical kerning, InDesign uses a different approach: It calculates the kerning values based on the optical appearance of the character shapes. This can often better handle situations where fonts and sizes are mixed. To apply Optical kerning, select a range of characters with the Type tool (or one or more unlinked text frames with the Selection tool), then choose Optical in the Kerning popup menu. The menu displays "Optical," for the selected text, but if you click an insertion point between two characters, InDesign shows you the actual kerning value.

Tracking

You can set tracking values in InDesign by selecting a range of text and using the Tracking menu in the Character or Control palette or with keystrokes (hold down Option/Alt and press either the left or right arrow keys on your keyboard). Tracking is measured in thousandths of an em, and can be used in a style. Note that InDesign lacks XPress's tracking tables function.

Type Styles

InDesign shares the same sorts of styles that QuarkXPress and PageMaker offers, such as bold and italic (see Table 22-1), though you apply some of them differently than in the other applications. In addition, InDesign has two new character-level attributes—ligatures and no break.

Font Styling

InDesign controls its own font menus, and only type styles which actually exist in the font appear in the Font Family menu on the Character or Control palette and in the Font menu under the Type menu. To choose font styling (Plain, Bold, Italic, and so on), pick a typeface from one of these popup menus or submenus, or use a keyboard shortcut.

If you press the keyboard shortcut for bold or italic, InDesign will only apply the style if those font styles actually exist. However, these shortcuts may not work the same with every font. For example, Sumner Stone, the designer of Adobe's Stone Sans, Stone Serif and Stone Informal families, decided that the Bold command should call out the semibold weight of the font instead of the bold weight.

Underline and Strikethrough

InDesign offers very fine control over underlines and strikethroughs. Choose Underline Options or Strikethrough Options from the Character or Control Palette menu (or Option/Alt-click on the underline and strikethrough icons in the Control palette) to choose weight, linc type, offset, color, and tint.

All Caps and Small Caps

InDesign includes the same All Caps and Small Caps type styles that QuarkXPress and PageMaker have, but InDesign's implementation is more sophisticated. These type styles are found on the Character or Control palette's flyout menu. Applying the All Caps style does not change the case of the type, only its appearance (to change the case, use the Change Case command described below). Applying the Small Caps style calls out the small cap glyphs if they exist in the font (as is the case with many "pro" OpenType fonts—see below). If they don't exist, InDesign synthesizes them using the settings in Text Preferences, reducing the text size.

If you apply the All Caps and Small Caps styles to OpenType fonts, it applies more typographically sophisticated changes. We discuss OpenType fonts in more detail later in this chapter.

Typography

Table 22-1 Type styles

To create this style...	Do this...	Or use this keystroke
Plain text	Use Font Family popup menu	Ctrl/Command-Shift-Y
Bold	Use Font Family popup menu	Ctrl/Command-Shift-B
Italic	Use Font Family popup menu	Ctrl/Command-Shift-I
Outline	Stroke the type	
Shadow	Use the Drop Shadow feature	Command-Option/Ctrl-Alt-M
Strikethrough	Use Character palette flyout menu	Ctrl/Command-Shift-forward slash
Underline	Use Character palette flyout menu	Ctrl/Command-Shift-U
Word underline	Style not supported	
Small caps	Use Character palette flyout menu	Ctrl/Command-Shift-H
All caps	Use Character palette flyout menu	Ctrl/Command-Shift-K
Superscript	Use Character palette flyout menu	Ctrl/Command-Shift-Equals
Subscript	Use Character palette flyout menu	Command-Option-Shift-Equals/ Ctrl-Alt-Shift-Equals
Superior	Style not supported; use Superscript	

Changing Case

In addition to the type styles described in the previous section, InDesign has Change Case commands in the Type menu. These aren't really type styles; they're more like functions you can use to change text characters. There are four Change Case commands: Uppercase, Lowercase, Title Case (capitalizes the first letter of each word), and Sentence case (capitalizes the first letter of each sentence).

Changing Position

InDesign has two type styles for positioning characters—superscript and subscript—both of which are found on the Character or Control palette flyout menu. You can set the preferences for the size and position for each of these in the Text panel of the Preferences dialog box.

If you're using an OpenType font which contains real superscript and subscript glyphs for the characters you're using, you can instead choose Superscript/Superior or Subscript/Inferior from the OpenType submenu (in the Character or Control palette's flyout menu).

Ligatures

A *ligature* is a character that combines two or more characters into one. The most common examples are the *fi* and *fl* ligatures which are part of the Macintosh font encoding (but not Windows). InDesign applies ligatures as a character attribute.

When you turn on ligatures (from the flyout menu in the Character or Control palette) with an OpenType font, InDesign uses any standard ligatures which the font designer has included in the font. Additionally, however, you can choose Discretionary Ligatures on the OpenType submenu, and turn on additional discretionary and historical ligatures which may be defined in the font.

No Break

When you want to keep a word or words from breaking in PageMaker or QuarkXPress, you can either use a discretionary hyphen or non-breaking spaces and hyphens. InDesign lets you use those methods, but also adds another option: You can keep a range of selected characters from breaking by applying the No Break type style, found on the Character or Control palette menu. When you use it, InDesign attempts to keep the selected characters on the same line.

Horizontal and Vertical Scaling

Horizontal or vertical scaling artificially compresses or expands characters, distorting their shapes. InDesign allows you to set horizontal and vertical scaling for type independently using controls on the Character or Control palette.

Color, Tint, Gradient, and Stroke

InDesign gives you the ability to set character color and tint ("shade" in XPress terminology) using the Swatches palette and the Color palette. In addition to applying color to text, InDesign also supports applying a gradient, and stroking text characters. We discuss these features in Chapter 38.

Baseline Shift

Baseline shift moves characters above or below the baseline, the imaginary line on which your type sits. In InDesign, you choose a value in the Baseline Shift field on the Character palette. Positive values shift characters above the baseline; negative values shift them below the baseline. To baseline shift selected text, either type in a value in points, or click the up/down arrows to increase or decrease the offset value in 1-point increments.

Skew

The *skew* type style lets you create a false italic (oblique) effect in a font which lacks that feature. You can apply this type style in InDesign by choosing a value in the Skew field on the Character or Control palette. Enter a skew angle in degrees, or click the up/down arrows to increase or decrease the angle in 1-degree increments.

Language

You may assign language as a character attribute. This is useful when you want to check spelling or hyphenate based on another language's dictionary (see Chapter 21).

OpenType Font Support

The biggest advance in fonts in the past decade is the advent of OpenType fonts, a new font format developed by Adobe and Microsoft and introduced in 2000. OpenType fonts have several advantages:

- They use a cross-plaform format and store their data in a single file so the same font can be used on the Macintosh or Windows platforms.

- They use in an industry-standard double-byte encoding called Unicode which can support over 65,000 glyphs. As a result, a single font can now contain all the characters for several different languages—and also contain the glyphs used in fine typography.

- They support high quality typography through the use of standardized layout tables. This makes it possible for an Open Type-smart application like InDesign to automatically call out these typographic features without extra effort.

You can access any font's special features with the OpenType submenu in the Character and Control palette's flyout menu. For example, you can choose Proportional Oldstyle to format numbers as oldstyle numerals. If you see a feature listed in square brackets, like "[Swash]," that feature isn't available in the current font. The OpenType User Guide, also included in the Goodies folder of the installation CD, gives detailed suggestions for using Adobe OpenType fonts. Some examples of fine typography produced with these fonts are shown in Figure 22-2.

Special Characters

To insert a special character in QuarkXPress or PageMaker, you're forced to memorize particular keystrokes, or perhaps rely on a crib sheet taped near your computer. By contrast, InDesign gives you several ways of calling out special characters—including two menus and a palette. However, you can still use keystrokes if you prefer. In addition, if you're using OpenType fonts, some special characters can be inserted in your text automatically.

Insert Character Menus
InDesign offers three special character submenus under the Type menu: Insert Special Character, Insert White Space, or Insert Break Character. The menus list all the white space (such as em space and thin space) and break characters (like the page or column breaks), and many common special characters (such as a registration mark). Instead of going to the Type menu, you can insert special characters with the context menu: Use the Type tool to place the text insertion point, then Control-click/right-click and select a character from one of the three submenus.

Glyphs Palette
The Glyphs palette gives you access to all glyphs in a font. You can open the palette by placing the text cursor in a frame and choosing Glyphs from

the Type menu (see Figure 22-3). The palette displays the glyphs from the current font, though you can choose a different font from the Font Family and Type Style popup menus at the bottom of the palette. Click the Zoom buttons to enlarge or reduce the size of the glyphs. Then scroll through the palette to see all the characters. To insert a glyph you see in the Glyphs palette, double-click on it.

InDesign CS also gives you the ability to create and use Glyph Sets. These are sets of special characters which you'd like to use again. You can create, view, and edit glyph sets from the Glyphs palette flyout menu.

Keystrokes

Of course, the fastest way to get a special character is to memorize and type a keystroke. Many special characters already have shortcuts defined (see Chapter 5 for more on how to set, view, and edit shortcuts).

Other Special Characters

InDesign can automatically substitute one character with another when appropriate. This is especially useful for ligatures, fractions, and so on.

Figure 22-2
Faked styles (left)
versus OpenType
features (right)

CURIOUSER AND CURIOUSER	CURIOUSER AND CURIOUSER	Small caps
1⅛ 3½ 5¹¹/₁₂ 8²³⁴/₅₆₇	1⅛ 3½ 5¹¹/₁₂ 8²³⁴/₅₆₇	Fractions
new azaleas bloom where	*new azaleas bloom where*	Contextual alternates

Figure 22-3
Glyphs palette

Typography

Fractions

InDesign has no macro like XPress's Type Tricks XTension, so making fractions with non-OpenType fonts is a hassle. (You can use the Superscript and Subscript styles and the fraction-bar character, or use specialized fonts.) However, many OpenType fonts support some pre-built fractions, and some (mostly the Pro fonts) even support the creation of any arbitrary fraction (like $355/113$). To use this feature, select any two numbers separated by a slash character—for example, 3/4—then select Fractions from the OpenType menu on the Character palette. The fractions will be correctly built using numerator and denominator characters included in the font.

Typographers' Quotes

InDesign have preferences that control the appearance of single and double quotation marks in text. By default, InDesign converts quotes to typographers' ("curly") quotes, but you can turn this off in the Text panel of the Preferences dialog box.

Quotation marks are also converted to typographer's quotes when text is imported with the Place command. To turn this off, uncheck the Convert Quotes option in the Import Options dialog box.

Auto Page Numbers and Jump Lines

The Insert Special Character submenu includes three characters used to reference pages in a document. The Auto Page Number is usually placed on master pages to create page numbers. The other two characters—Previous Page Number and Next Page Number—are used when stories jump from page to page, as they often do in newsletters or magazines. In InDesign, it usually works best to place these characters in a separate frame for a jump line (for example, Continued on Page x). Position the jump line so it overlaps the main story frame, and then it can correctly call out the page you're jumping to or from. All three characters work exactly the same way as in XPress.

23

Paragraph Formatting

As you work with text, you organize characters into words and words into paragraphs. When you work on a paragraph level, you shape the way text looks by defining its horizontal alignment, spacing, indents and tabs, baseline grid, text composition, hyphenation and justification, and you create attributes like drop caps and rules.

Selecting Paragraphs

InDesign provides several ways to select text when you're using paragraph formatting:

- As in XPress and PageMaker, you can place the text insertion point anywhere in the paragraph; you don't have to select the whole paragraph. Similarly, you can select a range of text in a text frame with the Type tool. Formatting applies to paragraphs included in the range, even if you don't select all the text in a paragraph.

- Unlike XPress or PageMaker, you can use the Selection tool to select one or more unlinked text frames. Formatting applies to all the text in the selected frames.

- In addition, paragraph attributes can be copied with the Eyedropper tool and applied to other type (see Chapter 38).

Alignment and Spacing

Some alignment and spacing choices are tied to the text frame. These include inset spacing, first baseline, and vertical alignment; we discuss these in Chapter 24. For now, we'll discuss how to control space within and around paragraphs.

You can control paragraph formatting in the Paragraph palette (see Figure 23-1) or the Control palette. If the Paragraph palette isn't open, you can choose Paragraph from the Type menu (or press Command-M/Ctrl-M, which also selects the Left Indent field in the palette). To see all the palette's choices, choose Show Options from the palette menu.

Leading

If you're expecting us to talk about leading as a paragraph attribute here, you're looking in the wrong place! InDesign, by default, considers leading to be a character attribute, although you can make it apply to an entire paragraph (see Chapter 22).

Horizontal Alignment

Five of the seven horizontal alignment buttons in InDesign's Paragraph palette duplicate the alignments in PageMaker and XPress. The last two offer new options: setting the last line of justified text center aligned or right aligned. We usually use the keystrokes we know from QuarkXPress or PageMaker: You can hold down the Command-Shift/Ctrl-Shift keys,

Figure 23-1

The Paragraph palette

A *Align left*	J *First line indent*
B *Align center*	K *Do not align to baseline grid*
C *Align right*	L *Align to baseline grid*
D *Justify with last line aligned left*	M *Space before*
E *Justify with last line aligned center*	N *Space after*
F *Justify with last line aligned right*	O *Drop cap number of lines*
G *Justify all lines*	P *Drop cap number of characters*
H *Left indent*	Q *Hyphenate checkbox*
I *Right indent*	

and press L for left, C for center, R for right, J for justified (last line aligned left). The only difference is the shortcut for force justifying all lines: Command-Shift-F/Ctrl-Shift-F.

Left and Right Indents

InDesign shares the same basic paragraph indent commands as Quark-XPress or PageMaker—left indent, right indent, and first line indent—each of which you can set in InDesign's Paragraph, Control, or Tabs palette.

By default, indent values are displayed in the units shown on the horizontal ruler, but you may use any measurement units InDesign supports: Type *i, in,* or " for inches, *pt* for points, *p* for picas, *mm* for millimeters, *cm* for centimeters, or *c* for ciceros.

If you like working interactively rather than numerically, you can set your indents on InDesign's Tabs palette (see Figure 23-2). To open the palette, choose Tabs from the Type menu or press Command-Shift-T/Ctrl-Shift-T. We explore the Tabs palette below; here we'll just discuss its indent features. Use one of these methods to position indents:

- Drag the top marker on the left side to indent the first line. Drag the bottom marker on the left to move both left markers and set the left indent for the paragraph. Drag the right marker to set the right indent. As you move these markers, InDesign displays their numeric position in the Position (X) field.

- Click on one of the indent markers to select it, type an indent value in the Position (X) field, then press Enter.

Hanging Indents

Creating hanging indents is one of the most common ways of formatting text: It's used whenever you want to create a numbered or bulleted list, for example.

Figure 23-2
The Tabs palette showing the first line indent set at 0.5 inches.

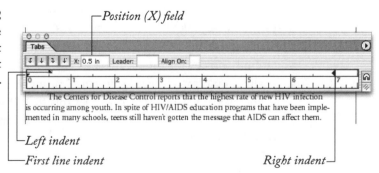

Position (X) field

Left indent

First line indent

Right indent

The first way to create a hanging indent effect is by typing a negative number in the First Line Indent field of the Paragraph or Control palette. For example, if you want to create a hanging indent where a bulleted list hangs in .25 inch, set the Left Indent value to ".25 in" and the First Line Indent to "−.25 in" . You can only use a negative first-line indent when there is an equal or greater left indent.

You can also create a hanging indent with the Tabs palette. In the Tabs palette, either drag the indent markers, or type indent values in the Position (X) field with a negative value for the First Line Indent. If you're dragging, hold down the Shift key to drag the lower-left marker (the Left Indent value) without moving the First Line indent marker.

The Indent Here Character

InDesign has also adopted the Indent Here Character from QuarkXPress. Typing Command-backslash/Ctrl-backslash causes the text on the remaining lines of the paragraph to indent to the same horizontal position as the Indent Here character. You can use the Indent Here character to create a type effect like a hung initial cap, for example, or to make a quick bulleted or numbered list. However, we don't find this very useful for hanging indents because this character can't be built into a paragraph style (while setting the First Line and Left Indent values can).

Space Before and After

InDesign's Space Before and Space After fields (in the Paragraph or Control palette) act exactly the same as PageMaker or QuarkXPress. You can either type a value into the fields and press Enter, place the cursor in one of these fields and press the Up/Down Arrow keys, or click the up/down arrows next to the field. Space Before has no effect at the top of a column of text and Space After has no effect at the bottom of a column of text.

Baseline Grid

InDesign supports using a document-wide baseline grid to align paragraphs, just as QuarkXPress and PageMaker do. The settings which control the baseline grid are in the Grids panel of the Preferences dialog box. There you'll find choices for the grid color, start value, and increment, which normally should match the document's leading. You can also set a View Threshold value. For example, if you set this to 100%, the baseline grid is invisible at magnifications lower than 100%, but appears when you are zoomed in.

If you want to anchor a paragraph to the baseline grid, click the Align to Baseline Grid icon on the Paragraph or Control palette (or press Command-Option-Shift-G/Ctrl-Alt-Shift-G to turn it on or off). To remove the anchoring, click the Do Not Align to Baseline Grid icon. You can display or hide the baseline grid from the View menu or by pressing Command-Option-'/Ctrl-Alt-' (quote mark).

Note that InDesign offers a unique feature: The ability to align just the first paragraph to the baseline grid. This is often useful for sidebars and pullquotes. To do this, align the paragraph to the baseline grid and then choose Only Align First Line to Grid from the flyout menu in the Paragraph or Control palette.

Drop Caps

Drop caps work identically in InDesign and XPress, though here you set them in either the Paragraph or the Control palette. The palette contains two drop cap fields: Number of Lines and Number of Characters. To adjust the space between a drop cap and the text which follows, adjust the kerning between the drop cap and the next character.

Keep Options

The Keep Options dialog box helps you eliminate widows and orphans in text as well as control how paragraphs stay together. You can find these choices by choosing Keep Options on the Paragraph or Control palette's flyout menu, or by pressing Command-Option-K/Ctrl-Alt-K. These options are very similar to XPress's, with an addition of the Start Paragraph feature.

Keep with Next
The Keep with Next option lets you specify how many lines (up to five) of the following paragraph must stay with the current paragraph. Usually you'll use this to keep a heading with the paragraph which follows it.

Keep Lines Together
The Keep Lines Together feature has identical choices to those in XPress: All Lines in Paragraph and Lines At Start/End of Paragraph. By using these options you can control orphans and widows by deciding whether all lines in a paragraph are kept together, or just a couple of beginning and ending lines.

Typography

Start Paragraph

The Start Paragraph menu lets you force a paragraph to begin in the next column, frame, page, or even the next odd or even page.

Working with Tabs

Unlike QuarkXPress, which affixes a temporary ruler at the top of the text box whenever the Tab dialog box is open, InDesign's Tabs feature uses a palette. To work with tabs in InDesign, open the Tabs palette by choosing Tabs from the Type menu (or press Command-Shift-T/Ctrl-Shift-T; see Figure 23-2, earlier in this chapter). If you want the ruler to align with the text frame, change your view to show the top of the text frame at its full width, select the frame with the Selection tool or the Type tool, and then click the magnet button on the right side of the palette. The palette should jump into position at the top of the frame. However, note that you don't have to align the ruler in order set tab stops.

Creating Tab Stops

To add a tab stop, first select the paragraphs which you want to affect (either use the Type tool to select one or more paragraphs or use the Selection tool to choose an unlinked text frame). Next, click one of the four tab alignment buttons in the Tabs palette to set the alignment of the tab stop. Then do one of the following:

- Click in the tab ruler where you want the tab stop to appear (click in the narrow space just above the ruler).

- Type a value in the Position (X) field and press Enter.

By the way, you don't have to align the Tabs palette with the text frame because when you click and drag a tab stop in the palette, InDesign displays a vertical line over the text frame reflecting the position of the tab stop. It's a little thing, but it saves so much time. Try it!

Tab Alignment

Tab stops can either be aligned by pressing one of the tab alignment buttons before creating a tab stop, or by selecting a tab stop and clicking a button. InDesign uses four kinds of tab stops: Left, Center, Right, and Align On. The Align On button can handle alignment on a decimal point (period), comma, or any other character. Type or paste the character you wish to align on into the Align On Character field and press Enter.

Tab Leaders

What QuarkXPress calls fill characters, InDesign calls tab leaders. To add a one or more characters to fill the space created by the tab, select a tab stop and enter one or more characters in the Tab Leader field, then press Enter. XPress is limited to two fill characters, but InDesign allows as many as eight. You can also format the tab character by selecting it (the "space" itself) with the Type tool and using the Character or Control palette.

Changing and Deleting Tabs

Once you have created tab stops, you can change or delete them. To move a tab stop, select it on the tab ruler (click on it). Then either drag it to a new position, or type a new value in the Position (X) field and press Enter. To remove a tab stop, drag it off the tab ruler. If you want to remove all the tabs, choose Clear All from the Tabs palette's flyout menu.

Single-line vs. Paragraph Composers

Composition is the complex process of fitting words into lines by weighing the hyphenation and justification settings (which we discuss in detail on the next page) and the break-points specified in hyphenation dictionaries (which we discuss in Chapter 21).

Single-line composers—like the ones in QuarkXPress and Page-Maker—only set one line of type at a time, ignoring the lines above and below it. The result of this process is that, while many lines may look fine, some lines in a paragraph will be looser or tighter, giving an overall unevenness to the "color" of justified type.

InDesign includes a single-line composer, too, but by default it uses a "paragraph composer," which almost always sets better-looking type (see Figure 23-3). The paragraph composer has a more complex job: While it uses the same rules for hyphenation and justification as the single-line composer, it looks through all the words of the paragraph in deciding how lines should end. It evaluates a complex network of choices—sometimes looking backward—and moves words up and down between lines until the best overall appearance is reached. You can see this process when typing in InDesign. As you type, words you already have typed are shifted up and down, or hyphenated.

Most of the time, you'll probably want to compose your type using the Adobe Paragraph Composer, which is InDesign's default choice. Occasionally, you may want to try the single-line composer. You can choose among the two composers in the Paragraph palette's flyout menu.

Figure 23-3

Single-line and
Paragraph composer

So she was considering in her own mind (as well as she could, for the hot day made her feel very sleepy and stupid), whether the pleasure of making a daisy-chain would be worth the trouble of getting up and picking the daisies, when suddenly a White Rabbit with pink eyes ran close by her.

There was nothing so *very* remarkable in that; nor did Alice think it so *very* much out of the way to hear the Rabbit say to itself, "Oh dear! Oh dear! I shall be late!" (when she thought it over afterwards, it occurred to her that she ought to have wondered at this, but at the time it all seemed quite natural); but when the Rabbit actually *took a watch out of its waistcoat-pocket,* and looked at it, and then hurried on, Alice started to her feet, for it flashed across her mind that she had never before seen a rabbit with either a waistcoat-pocket, or a watch

*Single–line composition
in QuarkXPress*

So she was considering in her own mind (as well as she could, for the hot day made her feel very sleepy and stupid), whether the pleasure of making a daisy-chain would be worth the trouble of getting up and picking the daisies, when suddenly a White Rabbit with pink eyes ran close by her.

There was nothing so *very* remarkable in that; nor did Alice think it so *very* much out of the way to hear the Rabbit say to itself, "Oh dear! Oh dear! I shall be late!" (when she thought it over afterwards, it occurred to her that she ought to have wondered at this, but at the time it all seemed quite natural); but when the Rabbit actually took a watch out of its waistcoat-pocket, and looked at it, and then hurried on, Alice started to her feet, for it flashed across her mind that she had never before seen a rabbit with either a waistcoat-pocket, or a watch to take out of it, and burning with curiosity, she ran

*Paragraph composition
in InDesign*

Hyphenation and Justification

Hyphenation and justification—usually called "H&J" by those who love fine typography—are the controls (along with the dictionaries we talk about in Chapter 21) which your composition engine uses to decide how much text to fit on a line. InDesign uses two separate dialog boxes to control H&J—Justification and Hyphenation—which are each found on the Paragraph or Control palette's flyout menu.

Applying H&J Settings

PageMaker, QuarkXPress, and InDesign all let you control H&J at the paragraph level, but the way the settings are applied differs among programs. Specifically, InDesign doesn't let you save H&J settings, as XPress does. Rather, you apply H&J settings in the following ways:

- To apply settings to particular paragraphs, select the paragraphs and make your choices in the two dialog boxes.

- To create default settings within a document, make choices in the Hyphenation and Justification dialog boxes with nothing selected. All subsequently created text frames will use these settings.

- To create default settings which apply to all new documents, make the choices in these two dialog boxes with no document open.

- The most efficient way to apply multiple H&J settings in a document is to include them in paragraph styles (see Chapter 26).

Hyphenation Settings

If you simply want to turn hyphenation on or off, select one or more paragraphs with the Type tool (or choose text frames with the Selection tool) and then check or uncheck the Hyphenation option in the Paragraph or Control palette. However, to fine-tune the settings InDesign uses for hyphenation, choose Hyphenation from the Paragraph palette's flyout menu to show the Hyphenation dialog box (see Figure 23-4). Most of the options there are similar to those in PageMaker and XPress.

One feature in this dialog box that those other programs *don't* offer is the *hyphenation penalty slider*. If you move the slider to the left toward Better Spacing, the composer relies more on hyphenation and less on adjusting spacing. If you drag the slider to the right toward Fewer Hyphens, it makes more adjustments with spacing, and use fewer hyphenation break-points. Be sure to turn on the Preview checkbox so you can see the effect on your selected paragraphs.

Figure 23-4
The Hyphenation
dialog box

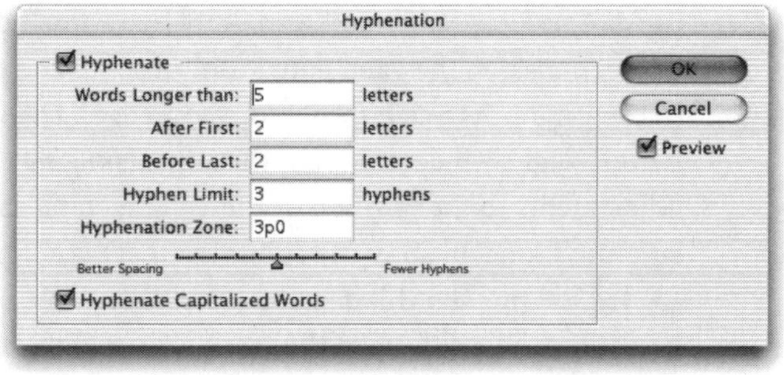

Justification Settings

Justification controls the spacing of letters and words across the text column by setting a range of acceptable spacing which the composition engine can use. You can adjust these settings in the Justification dialog box, also found on the Paragraph or Control palette's flyout menu (see Figure 23-5).

QuarkXPress and PageMaker let you set Minimum, Optimum, and Maximum values for Space (word spacing) and Character (character spacing), all set as a percentage of a normal space character. InDesign has equivalent controls, called Minimum, Desired, and Maximum Word Spacing and Letter Spacing, each also set as a percentage.

In addition, InDesign gives you the ability to alter Glyph Scaling, which lets you subtly change the width (horizontal scaling) of the characters. If you set a modest Glyph Scaling value—like Minimum 98-percent and Maximum 102-percent—the difference in letterform shapes probably won't be distinguishable. It's also useful to use the Preview option to test out spacing alternatives before applying them or including them in a paragraph style.

Figure 23-5

The Justification dialog box

Hanging Punctuation

People who love well-set type are always concerned about the "look" of the type. One high-quality "look" which has largely disappeared over the past decade of desktop publishing is when the edges along each side of a column of text appear even. Normally, when some punctuation marks—periods, commas, dashes, and quotations marks—and the edges of some letters (like a capital A) touch the left or right edge of a text frame, they appear to be very slightly indented from the edge. *Hanging punctuation* makes subtle adjustments to the position of these characters, moving them slightly outside the frame, making the column appear straighter and cleaner.

InDesign calls this feature *optical character alignment,* and it implements it as an attribute of the story. To apply this effect to your text, select a text frame with the Selection tool or click an insertion point with the Type tool, open the Story palette (choose Story from the Type menu), and turn on the Optical Margin Alignment option. The hanging effect applies to all linked frames in your story.

Paragraph Rules

Paragraph rules are a paragraph attribute which places lines above, below, and sometimes through the text of a paragraph. You can add a paragraph rule using a dialog box or in a paragraph style. In InDesign, select one or more paragraphs with the Type tool, and then choose Paragraph Rule from the Paragraph or Control palette's flyout menu (or press Command-Option-J/Ctrl-Alt-J). The Paragraph Rules dialog box appears. Unfortunately, while InDesign allows you to set both a Rule Above and a Rule Below in the same paragraph, you must select one or the other from the popup menu, and you can only look at the settings for one at a time.

In InDesign, you can set the Weight, Line Type, Color, Tint, Gap Color and Tint. InDesign lets you use any color you've created in the Swatches palette, including gradients, and to set overprinting strokes.

Positioning the Rules

There are two attributes used when positioning a rule or rules in a paragraph: The vertical position (the "Offset") and the horizontal position.

InDesign, unlike XPress, only allows absolute positioning of the rules. The offset for Rule Above is measured from the baseline of the top line of the text to bottom of the rule. The offset for Rule Below is measured from the baseline of the last line of text to the top of the rule.

You may set a paragraph rule to be the width of the text or the column—a choice you make in the Width popup menu—and adjust that based on the Left and Right Indent values. The column is defined by the both text frame and the Text Inset value (from the Text Frame Options dialog box; see the next chapter).

Typography

24

Text Frame Properties

While most text attributes are controlled on the character and paragraph level, there is a third way you can change text appearance—by setting the properties of the frame which contains the text.

Fitting a Frame to Its Text

Before we discuss those controls, let's introduce a useful technique for fitting text in its frame. Text frames are often larger than they need to be. You can ask InDesign to automatically fit the frame to the size of the text contained in it. First, either select the frame or frames with the Selection tool or click an insertion point with the Type tool. Then choose Fit Frame to Content from the Fitting submenu (under the Object menu), or press Command-Option-C/Ctrl-Alt-C.

The frame's size is reduced to the size of the text, but how it happens depends on what it contains.

- If the text is only one line, InDesign changes both the height and width of the frame. (This is useful for captions!)

- If the text is more than one line, InDesign reduces the height, but not the width of the frame.

- If the frame contains only a table, InDesign reduces or expands the text frame to fit the table (height and width).

Note that you'll find the Fit Frame to Content command useless if the frame is linked to other frames or if text is overset (text frames are never made larger). We discuss similar commands for working with fitting graphics in Chapter 29.

Text Frame Options

To set text frame attributes, either choose the frame or frames with the Selection tool, or place the text insertion point in the frame with the Type tool. Then choose Text Frame Options from the Object menu (or press Command-B/Ctrl-B; see Figure 24-1). Here's one more way to get here: Option/Alt-double-click on the text frame with the Selection tool.

Throughout the dialog box, you can either type in values, click the tiny up/down arrow buttons, or press the up or down arrow keys on your keyboard to increase or decrease the values—the amount of change depends on the ruler unit selected.

Columns

InDesign, like QuarkXPress, lets you set the number of columns in a text frame, as well as the gutter width (width between columns). But InDesign goes one step farther: It lets you define the width of a column. If you do this, as you adjust column and gutter widths, the width of the text frame changes, too. If you want to make sure the text column width doesn't change, you can turn on the Fixed Column Width option. With this on, resizing the text frame leaves the column width unchanged, but changes the *number* of columns.

Figure 24-1
Text Frame Options
dialog box

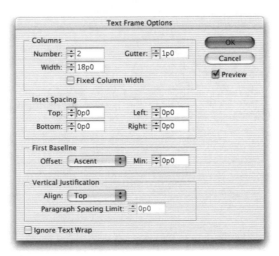

Inset Spacing

Text inset defines the amount of space from the edge of the frame to the text in the frame. InDesign allows you to set the Top, Bottom, Left and Right inset values independently. InDesign's default is an inset value of 0 (zero), rather than the 1-point value in XPress which has always annoyed us. When it comes to non-rectangular frames, you can specify only one inset value.

Vertical Text Alignment

If you're familiar with QuarkXPress, you know that it has two ways of adjusting text vertically in a box: by setting the First Baseline Offset and by choosing a Vertical Justification option in the Modify dialog box. InDesign closely matches these choices in the Text Frame Options dialog box.

You can set the distance from the top of the frame to the first baseline of text by choosing the Minimum amount for baseline offset, and then choose between Cap Height, Ascent, Leading (the text's leading value), x Height (the height of the "x" character of the font), or Fixed.

Both XPress and InDesign also let you choose between Top, Centered, Bottom and Justified vertical alignment within a text frame. XPress has a choice to set the Inter ¶ Max when Justified is selected—the maximum distance between paragraphs. In InDesign, the same option is called Paragraph Spacing Limit. As with XPress, vertical justification isn't allowed when a frame isn't rectangular or when an object with text wrap is causing runaround.

25

Find and Change

The Find/Change and Find Font commands are two of the workhorses of a page layout program. These features are rarely mentioned in application feature lists, but learning how to use tem well can save you a huge amount of time. In InDesign, the Find/Change function is controlled with a dialog box which acts as a palette (so it can be left open as you work; see Figure 25-1). In InDesign, you open it by choosing Find/Change in the Edit menu (or press Command-F/Ctrl-F).

Setting the Search Range

Like XPress and PageMaker, InDesign lets you search the current story or the current document. InDesign can also search a text selection, multiple stories, or even all your open documents. In the Search popup menu, select the range to be searched: Selection, Story, Stories, To End of Story, Document, or All Documents. (The choices are context sensitive, so Stories is only available if you have more than one story selected with the Selection tool.) Note that searching a document also searches the master pages (in XPress, you have to do that as a separate search).

Specifying the Text

After setting the search range, type or paste the characters to be searched for in the Find What field. InDesign remembers the last 15 searches you've performed, and you can select them in the Previous Search popup menu (just to the right of the field). If you want to replace characters, type or

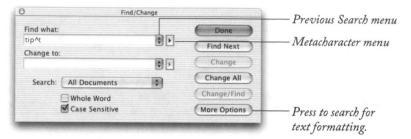

Figure 25-1
The Find/Change
dialog box in
its minimized
configuration, used
for character searches

Previous Search menu

Metacharacter menu

Press to search for text formatting.

paste the characters into the Change To field. This field also has a Previous Search menu with previous replacement characters.

To search and replace special characters—like auto page numbers or discretionary hyphens—you can choose them from the Metacharacter popup menu, to the right of the Find What and Change To fields. InDesign also has four wildcard characters: Any White Space Character (like a tab or space), Any Character, Any Digit, and Any Letter. These are also listed in the Metacharacters popup menu.

Both QuarkXPress and InDesign offer two more options when performing a Find/Change. When you check Whole Word, the search is limited to entire words only. Turning on the Case Sensitive option is the same as turning *off* Ignore Case in XPress.

Performing a Text Search

The buttons available in the Find/Change dialog box are Find Next, Change, Change/Find or Change All. When you are finished searching, click Done or click the close palette button.

Finding/Changing Formatted Text

To find or change formatted text in InDesign, click the More Options button in the Find/Change dialog box. InDesign now presents the expanded form of the dialog box showing its Format controls. You can then click the Format buttons to choose the formatting you wish to find or replace.

When you click one of the Format buttons, you see the Find Format Settings or Change Format Settings dialog box, which lets you specify the attributes which you want to find/change. You can Find/Change style sheets, basic and advanced character attributes, indents, spacing, keep options, drop caps, composer, character color, and OpenType features. (You can't Find/Change paragraph rules, tabs, or H&J settings.)

Formatting attributes in this dialog box can have one of three states—on, off, or ignore—representing whether the search is finding or changing text with or without this attribute, or whether this attribute is to be ignored.

Applying Formatting

After making choices for finding or changing formatting in the dialog box, click OK. When you return to the Find/Change dialog box, the formatting you've specified is listed in the Find Format Settings and Change Format Settings sections. When you are satisfied with your choices, use the Find Next, Change, Change/Find or Change All buttons as described above.

While XPress cannot undo a search and replace, InDesign can: choose Undo from the Edit menu or press Command-Z/Ctrl-Z. One common mistake is to inadvertently leave formatting attributes from a previous search. InDesign helps you recognize that formatting is being searched for or replaced by placing a yellow Formatting Alert icon next to the field where formatting is designated. To clear the formatting, press Clear.

Find Font Dialog Box

The Find Font dialog box (see Figure 25-2) allows you to see where in your document missing fonts are located, to replace fonts with other fonts on your system, or to gather information about the fonts in your document. The button labeled Less Info toggles with More Info to open or close the bottom portion of the dialog box.

InDesign can find or replace fonts on master pages at the same time as document pages. Furthermore, the Find Font dialog box also lists fonts which are located in EPS or PDF files (but it cannot replace them).

Finding Information

When you select a document font in the list, you can click the Find First button to find the first instance of the font in the document. The text that uses the document moves into view. If the font is in a graphic, the Find Font button changes to Find Graphic.

InDesign indicates in the font list whether a font is PostScript Type 1, TrueType or OpenType by its icon. If the lower portion of the dialog box is open, clicking on a font provides more information—the PostScript name, the location of the font, and the number of characters using the font, for instance. (The font type may be Unknown if the file format of the graphic doesn't provide information about the font.)

Figure 25-2

The Find Font dialog box in its expanded (More Info) state

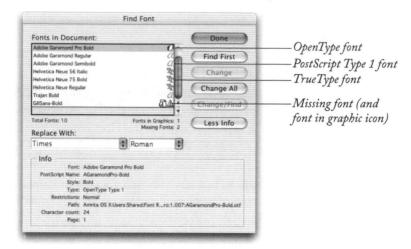

OpenType font
PostScript Type 1 font
TrueType font

Missing font (and font in graphic icon)

Replacing a Font

To replace a font, select it and then select a replacement font from the two Replace With popup menus. Click Find First, and then you can do one of the following:

- Click Change to change that instance of the font.

- Click Change/Find to change that instance and find the next instance.

- Click Change All to change all instances of the fonts selected in the list.

When all the instances of a font are removed, the font disappears from the list. InDesign shares QuarkXPress's limitation that font replacements don't change the fonts which are defined in a paragraph or character style. They apply the font change locally to the text, but they don't change the font in the style itself. This is, in our humble opinion, extremely annoying in both programs.

Note that to replace fonts which are in graphics, you have to open the application which originally exported the graphic, then update the graphic in InDesign.

PART 6

Styles

Paragraph Styles \ Styles \ atches

about cyber - head

Address street

ADDRESS1

big head

body

bold description

26

Paragraph and Character Styles

You'll be happy to know that InDesign styles meet or beat the capabilities of the paragraph and character styles in both QuarkXPress and PageMaker. However, it handles character styles in a very different way than XPress docs (PageMaker doesn't offer character-based styles). Also, InDesign splits styles into two separate palettes: Paragraph Styles and Character Styles. And unlike XPress, empty style palettes don't have any default styles, such as Normal.

Creating Paragraph Styles

To open the Paragraph Styles palette, choose Paragraph Styles from the Type menu or press its keyboard shortcut, F11. The fastest way to create a new style is to click the Create New Style button at the bottom of the Paragraph Styles palette (see Figure 26-1). However, you should hold down the Option/Alt key while you click, so you can name or define the style. You can also select New Style from the Paragraph Style palette's menu.

Use the New Paragraph Style dialog box to set up the style (see Figure 26-2). Select any of the panels along the left side of the dialog box to enter attributes for the style. InDesign lets you preview a style while modifying it by turning on the Preview checkbox in the lower left corner of this dialog box. When you're done setting up a style, click OK and the new style name appears in the Paragraph Styles palette.

You can duplicate an existing paragraph style by dragging the name of the original style on top of the New Style button.

Figure 26-1

You can create a new paragraph style by clicking (or Option/Alt-clicking) on the Create New Style button at the bottom of the Paragraph Styles palette. Or, as here, we drag another style on top of the button.

Figure 26-2

Defining a paragraph style

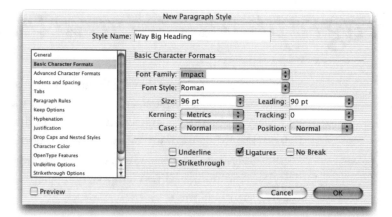

Just as in XPress and PageMaker, you can base one style on another. This simplifies production because the attributes in common between these styles are updated automatically when they're edited in the original style. You can set up a "based on" relationship in the General panel of the New Paragraph Style dialog box.

Character Styles

You can use InDesign's character styles to create, save, and apply a group of style attributes to a few selected words or characters (as opposed to an entire paragraph, which occurs when using paragraph styles). Creating, applying, and editing character styles generally works the same way as paragraph styles do, except they only apply to selected portions of text, so not all of the same attributes are available. Display the Character Styles palette using the command of the same name on the Type menu, or press Shift-F11.

InDesign only changes attributes that are specifically identified within a character style when it is applied. Leaving an attribute blank in the Character Styles palette will cause InDesign to not change that attribute of the text when the character style is used (see Figure 26-3).

Figure 26-3
Blank attributes mean "don't change this when I apply this style."

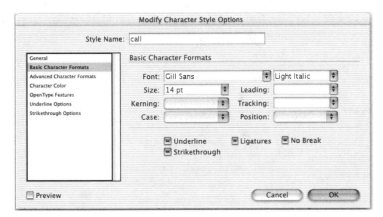

Applying paragraph and character styles using InDesign is very similar to both QuarkXPress and PageMaker. To apply a paragraph style, simply place the text cursor in a paragraph and then click on the name of the style in the Paragraph Styles palette (or choose from the style popup menu in the Control palette). Character styles take a bit more care to apply. As in XPress, you must first select the exact range of characters you want to change, and then select the style to be applied from the Character Styles or Control palette.

Applying Styles

You can also press a keyboard shortcut to apply a style if you've created a shortcut. With InDesign, you define keyboard shortcuts for styles using the Shortcut field in the General panel of the Modify Paragraph (or Character) Style Options dialog box. Note that InDesign only lets you combine a number on the numeric keypad with one or more modifier keys (such as Shift).

You can also copy both paragraph and character formatting using the Eyedropper tool when you don't feel it is necessary to build a Style.

Overriding Local Attributes

Any text formatting you use in addition to the given paragraph or character style is called *local formatting*. For example, making a single word italic is applying local formatting to it. InDesign adds a plus ("+") symbol to the style name displayed in the Styles palettes when the text insertion point is placed in styled text that has local formatting (see Figure 26-4).

InDesign does not change local formatting when you apply a character or paragraph style (for example, your italic words won't be changed). If you want to remove all local formatting, except character styles, hold down the Option/Alt key when you click the style you're applying. If you also hold down the Shift key, both local formatting and character styles are removed.

Figure 26-4
InDesign informs you of local formatting by placing a plus symbol after the style name.

Nested Styles

InDesign dramatically reduces the pain of applying two or more character styles in a paragraph when there is some definable structure, such as "apply one style to the first sentence, then a different style to the rest of the paragraph, except use a third style for the final word."

After creating one or more character styles, you can create this effect by choosing Drop Caps and Nested Styles from the flyout menu in the Paragraph or Control palette. Or, choose the Drop Caps and Nested Styles panel from the Paragraph Style Options dialog box (see Figure 26-5). Click the New Nested Style button and from the Nested Style drop-down menu, choose a character style. Then, choose how much of the paragraph start should be formatted by selecting how many words will be formatted or choose another method for defining the ending point of the character style, such as the first tab character. You can create multiple nested styles and use the arrow at the bottom of the dialog box to select a Nested Style and move it up or down in the list to determine which styles are applied first.

Modifying Styles

You can edit an existing style by double-clicking it in the Paragraph Styles or Character Styles palette. Either the Paragraph Style Options dialog box or the Character Style Options dialog box appears.

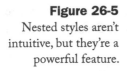

Figure 26-5
Nested styles aren't intuitive, but they're a powerful feature.

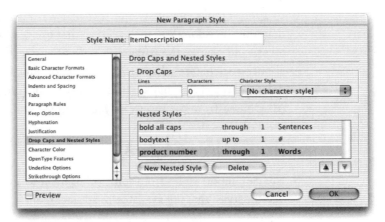

However, be very careful when editing styles: When you double-click on the style's name, you apply that style to any text you have selected (even if you have only selected a text frame with the Selection tool). This can cause much grief, believe us.

Fortunately, you can edit a style without affecting any text by holding down Command-Option-Shift/Ctrl-Alt-Shift while double-clicking the style name. Or you can make sure nothing on your page is selected by choosing Deselect All from the Edit menu (or press Command-Shift-A/Ctrl-Shift-A) prior to double-clicking the style you wish to edit. Or you can right-button click (Control-click on the Macintosh) on the style name in the palette to edit it without affecting selected text.

Redefining styles

Unlike XPress or PageMaker, you can actually change a style right on your document page instead of opening a dialog box. Select some text that is tagged with the style you want to change, then apply local formatting to it. While the text is selected, choose Redefine Style from the flyout menu on the Paragraph Styles or Character Styles palette. Or quicker: press Command-Option-Shift-R/Ctrl-Alt-Shift-R to redefine the paragraph style and Command-Option-Shift-C/Ctrl-Alt-Shift-C to redefine the character style.

Deleting Styles

You can delete a paragraph or character style by selecting it and clicking the trash icon in the Paragraph Styles or Character Styles palette, or choosing Delete Style from the palette's flyout menu. But before you delete a paragraph style, stop and think. When you delete a style you don't get a chance to apply a replacement style to text that was tagged with the style you're deleting. Therefore, you may want to first use the Find/Change palette to locate and change the paragraph style of any text that uses a style you're about to delete (see Chapter 25 for more on Find/Change). If you want to delete all the styles that are unused in your document, first choose Select All Unused from the palette's flyout menu.

Importing Styles

You can import styles from some other file into an InDesign file, or to the default styles that are available in all documents.

Importing Styles from a Document

You can append all of the paragraph and character styles from a saved InDesign document into your current document by selecting Load All Styles from the palette menu of either the Paragraph Styles or Character Styles palettes. Regardless of which palette you use to select this command, it imports both character and paragraph styles.

If you only want to import only the paragraph or only the character styles from another document, you can select Load Paragraph Styles from the Paragraph palette menu or Load Character Styles from the Character palette menu. Unfortunately, there is no way to specify *which* particular styles are imported (by name), as you can in XPress.

As in QuarkXPress and PageMaker, importing styles when no documents are open adds them to the list of default styles available in all new documents.

Importing Styles from Word Files

If you apply styles to your text while using a word processing program such as Microsoft Word, when you Place the text file into InDesign, the styles will come along, too. If the InDesign file doesn't have styles with the same names, then placing the text file imports those styles automatically.

Note that when you import text, you have the choice of turning on the Show Import Options checkbox in the Place dialog box. If Remove Text and Table Formatting is selected in the Import Options window, InDesign removes the formatting from the imported text (including the paragraph and character styles).

27

Exporting Text

As in QuarkXPress and PageMaker, you can export the text from your InDesign document separately from the document—either selected portions of a story or the entire text of the story (but only one story at a time). When you use this feature, only the text is saved to disk; graphics and inline objects aren't included.

You can use one of the following methods to export the text, depending on how much text you need to export:

- To export only a portion of text from a story, select that text, and then select Export from the File menu.

- To export an entire story (text flow), place your cursor in the story to be extracted (without actually selecting any text) and select Export from the File menu.

Either way, you then have to choose a file format from the Formats popup menu of the Export dialog box (see Figure 27-1).

Text Formats

When exporting text, you'll need to choose the export format for the text. Many of the formats (like PDF or JPEG) export an entire page or document instead of just your text, so choose carefully. The formats that only export text are listed below.

Figure 27-1
The Export
dialog box

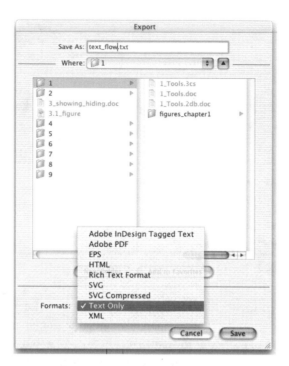

Text Only

Choose this option if you need the text to be usable on any computer operating system and any software. The Text Only option extracts the text and places it in a standard file format that virtually any text editing software will be able to read. Text Only removes any and all formatting you've applied to text and only exports the characters.

The Text Only option allows you to apply the characteristics of the computer platform where the files will be used, regardless of which computer operating system on which you are using InDesign (see Figure 27-2). By selecting Macintosh or PC, the text is structured so that characters will display and print properly when opened on the computer type you select. The Encoding option allows you to specify Unicode if necessary to preserve special characters.

Figure 27-2
The Text Only
export option

Rich Text Format

The Rich Text Format (RTF) saves your text with most of its formatting. You should use RTF if you're going to open the exported text file with Microsoft Word or place the text in an application that recognizes this file format, such as PageMaker or QuarkXPress for Windows.

Adobe InDesign Tagged Text

The most robust text-export format is InDesign Tagged Text, which is similar to XPress Tags. Tagged text saves all your text formatting, but only InDesign and Adobe InCopy can read these files.

The InDesign Tagged Text format is similar to Text Only, except that codes are written into the text to identify how the characters and paragraphs will be formatted. You can produce formatted text in any text-editing software using the InDesign tags and then place the formatted version into an InDesign document.

Although many of the InDesign Tagged Text tags resemble the XPress Tags format (which allows for a similar capability in QuarkXPress), they are not interchangeable.

If you choose InDesign Tagged Text, you get to choose how the text and the tags should be saved (see Figure 27-3).

- Verbose writes the tags in a longer form. For example, <StrokeColor: Red> as opposed to the Abbreviated option which would write <sc:Red>. If a human will be reading or editing the tags, you should export using Verbose.

- ASCII is used for most PC systems and is the most common format for representing English characters.

- ANSI includes the ASCII characters and also special punctuation marks and symbols that are not included with the ASCII character set. The

Figure 27-3
InDesign Tagged
Text options

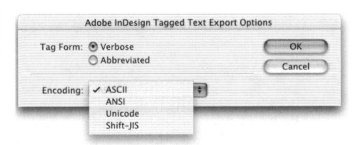

143

Macintosh operating system typically writes text using the ANSI format for plain text.

- Unicode can describe a much larger character set, including thousands of different glyphs, supporting non-European languages.

- Shift-JIS is used for Japanese characters that are to be represented as plain text.

For a detailed description of every code available using the InDesign Tagged Text export option, locate the Tagged Text.pdf file located on your Adobe InDesign CD. This file is also available for download from the Adobe Web site.

PART 7

Graphics

Links		
EdnasPoemsPart2.pdf	?	47
Big Hair.eps		50
eyeglasses.gray.psd		47

28

Importing Graphics

You can import graphics into your InDesign documents in very similar ways that you work in QuarkXPress or PageMaker, but InDesign also offers some new ways for you to be more creative and efficient when building your pages. For instance, it supports more flexible ways of creating graphic frames and a wider range of import options.

Placing Graphics

As in XPress or PageMaker, you can build placeholder frames on your page and import graphics into these frames. In QuarkXPress, you would use the Get Picture command to import a graphic. Instead, InDesign borrows from PageMaker: To select an image, choose Place from the File menu (or press Command-D/Ctrl-D).

As we discuss in Chapter 6, any frame may contain any content—you do not need to build frames specifically for text or pictures. If you don't want to replace the currently-selected picture or text, or anchor the image in your text, then turn off the Replace Selected Item option in the Place dialog box. This way, InDesign ignores the selected item and simply loads the Place gun. (If you forget and the image does replace a frame's content, you can press Command-Z/Ctrl-Z to undo and reload the Place gun.)

The Place Gun
As in PageMaker, you can choose the Place command even if you have not preselected a frame. Once you have selected a graphic in the Place dialog box and click OK, the Place command changes your cursor into either

a paint brush or an Acrobat cursor (the latter if you choose a PDF file), indicating that it is ready to place a graphic (see Figure 28-1). You can then move this "loaded graphic cursor"—also called the "Place gun"—over any empty frame. When you see parentheses around the cursor, click to place the image into the frame.

You can also create a frame at the same time you are importing a graphic. Either click and drag with the Place gun to manually define the frame size, or click once and InDesign builds a frame to the size of the image bounding box. This freedom lets you actually build a page at the same time you are importing images, so it is no longer necessary to create a dummy layout with empty boxes prior to importing the images.

Figure 28-1
The loaded graphic
"place gun" cursor

When you put the Place gun over a frame, it changes slightly.

Drag & Drop Importing

You can also select one or more files from your desktop or Windows Explorer and simply drag the files into InDesign. If you drag in a single image, you can drag the picture onto any empty frame on the page (even if it's not selected) to place the graphic inside that frame.

Graphic File Formats

Because you may be creating documents for different purposes, and because your artwork may be coming from a variety of sources, InDesign allows you to import 14 different graphic file formats. Anything PageMaker or QuarkXPress can import, InDesign can, too, with the exception of a couple of little-used formats (like PhotoCD). However, InDesign lets you import two file formats that these applications do not: native Photoshop (.PSD) and Illustrator (.AI) files.

Advantages of Native File Formats

The ability to import Photoshop and Illustrator files (native files) without having to first save into flattened .EPS, .JPG, or .TIFF formats can significantly speed the creative process, as you can link in InDesign directly to the original Photoshop or Illustrator files. That way, InDesign can update immediately when you make changes to the graphic. This also means that you can simplify your workflow and only save a single version of each graphic file, rather than two (the original and the "for print" version).

Another advantage of placing native Photoshop and Illustrator files is that they can contain transparency which InDesign recognizes. (EPS files don't support transparency.) In some cases, this can eliminate the need for creating clipping paths, as we discuss in Chapter 31. InDesign CS even can import Photoshop files which contain spot colors—either multitones (duotones, tritones or quadtones) or files with spot channels.

To Import or Not to Import

The problem is that native Photoshop files—especially those with many layers—can be huge. It probably doesn't make sense to import ten 200 MB .PSD files into InDesign, because when it comes time to send your file to the printer, you have to send those Photoshop files, too. Printing these files isn't a problem (though it takes InDesign a little longer to print because it has to flatten the images before sending them to the printer), but managing them is.

If you're dealing with very large Photoshop files, it may make more sense for you to use a more-traditional "downsample, sharpen, flatten, convert-to-CMYK, then export as TIFF" workflow (see David's *Real World Photoshop* for more on Photoshop production issues). On the other hand, there's rarely a problem using smallish Photoshop files or native Illustrator files, as they're rarely unwieldy.

Recommended Prepress Formats

As we said earlier, InDesign can accept almost any graphic file format you'd want. There's no problem with your using flattened TIFF, EPS, and JPG files rather than native file formats. Here are a few tips that might be useful:

- **TIFF.** This is normally the format we use for saving bitmapped images (if we're not using a native .PSD format). TIFF files can even contain alpha channels or clipping paths created in Photoshop.

- **EPS.** The Encapsulated PostScript (EPS) file format usually contains a low-resolution, low-quality PICT or TIFF preview which, by default, InDesign uses to display the image on screen (like QuarkXPress or PageMaker). However, InDesign can also interpret the PostScript code in the EPS file and display a high-quality version on screen (see Chapter 30) or when printing to a non-PostScript printer.

Graphics

- **JPEG (.JPG).** The JPEG file format uses a "lossy" compression mechanism which can cause image quality to deteriorate significantly. InDesign can import and print JPEG files, but you should make sure you use a minimum of compression (maximum quality) or else you will likely see image degradation, especially artifacts appearing around sharp high-contrast edges.

- **PDF.** PDF is a very flexible and robust file format. We now generally prefer this over the EPS format for vector artwork, and it can act as a native Adobe Illustrator file format. Photoshop's PDF files can be flattened or layered, include vector and transparency information, and are often surprisingly small on disk.

- **DCS.** Desktop Color Separations (DCS), developed by Quark, is a version of the standard EPS format. InDesign CS can now composite Photoshop's DCS files at print time, but because InDesign can read spot colors in .PSD files, there is little reason to use DCS anymore.

Inappropriate File Formats

Just because InDesign can import and print some file formats doesn't mean you should run out and use them. Here's a list of file formats that InDesign supports, but which we recommend avoiding if you're doing prepress work: GIF, PNG, BMP, PICT, WMF, PCX, Scitex CT. (If you're doing multimedia work, exporting PDFs from InDesign for the Web, then some of these may be appropriate.)

Import Options

The options available when you place a graphic are dependent on the file format of the graphic you are placing. The import options appear in a new dialog box when the Show Import Options checkbox is turned on in the Place dialog box (or if it's off and you hold down the Shift key when clicking OK). Generally, the options you set remain in effect for that file format until you change them.

Here's a list of the primary image import options:

- **Apply Photoshop Clipping Path.** When you place a TIFF or Photoshop file which contains a clipping path, turning on this option applies the clipping path automatically. If you leave this off, you can still apply the clipping path later (see Chapter 31). Note that this option is available with EPS files, too, but it will likely get you in trouble if you turn it on because it makes it appear that you can edit that clipping path in InDesign when you really can't.

- **Color Settings.** There are three color management options which can be selected for individual graphics—Enable Color Management, Profile, and Rendering Intent.

- **Read Embedded OPI Image Links.** Available only for EPS files. We discuss this in Chapter 44.

- **Alpha Channel.** When you import a TIFF or PSD file that contains you can pick any alpha channel to specify background transparency.

- **Proxy Generation.** Available only for EPS files. Select Use TIFF or PICT Preview to use the embedded preview stored in the file or choose Rasterize the PostScript to have InDesign create a preview.

- **Place PDF Options.** InDesign lets you select which page of a multi-page PDF you want to import. The Crop popup menu lets you choose how much of a PDF page to place. The Preserve Halftone Screens option overrides InDesign's settings when the PDF contains halftone screens. When the Transparent Background option is chosen, the background of a PDF containing transparency is honored; if turned off, the background is opaque.

The Links Palette

InDesign uses the Links palette (see Figure 28-2) to list the placed graphics within your document, informing you whether any files have been modified or are missing. To open the Links palette, choose Links from the Window menu or press Command-Shift-D/Ctrl-Shift-D. The Links palette also

Figure 28-2
The Links palette

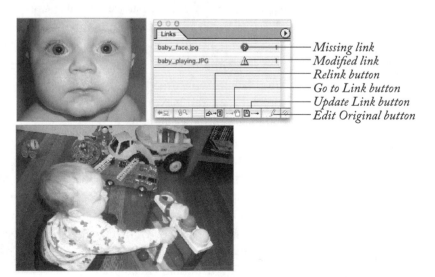

opens automatically if it detects a missing or modified file when you open a document; it then gives you the option of fixing the links immediately or waiting until later. The palette tracks all the linked graphics in your document. You can sort the list by name, page, or status by choosing these options on the palette's flyout menu.

Updating and Changing Graphic Links

If you have edited an image on disk, InDesign displays a yellow triangle icon adjacent to the its name in the Links palette. If you want InDesign to relink to the updated version, select the file's name in the Links palette and click the Update Link button or choose Update Link from the Links palette's flyout menu. It's easy to update all your graphics at once. Simply deselect all the linked graphic names by clicking in the blank space at the bottom of the palette. Then click the Update Link button, and all the modified graphics will be updated at once.

InDesign alerts you to images that it can no longer find on disk with a red stop sign icon in the Links palette. You can help InDesign locate the missing file by clicking the Relink button or choosing Relink from the palette's flyout menu. This command lets you then navigate to the new location of a file or specify a new file to use in place of the current file.

Information about Graphics

When you have lots of graphics spread across many pages, it can be hard find a specific image. Try this: Select a graphic on the palette, and tell InDesign to display the image by clicking the Go to Link button or selecting Go to Link from the palette's flyout menu.

InDesign displays information about each linked graphic—including file path, modification date, page number, color information, and file type—by either double-clicking on a graphic's name or choosing Link Information from the palette menu. In the Link Information dialog box, you can click the Next and Prev buttons to navigate through all your graphic links, and even relink to other graphics.

Editing the Original Graphic

A nice feature of InDesign is the ability to open an original graphic directly from the Links palette. To do this, select the graphic and click the Edit Original button. You can also select Edit Original from the flyout menu in the Links palette, by right-clicking (Control-click on the Mac) and choosing Edit Original from Graphics submenu in the context menu, or by Option/Alt-double-clicking on the image with the Selection tool.

Embedding Graphics

You can avoid the need to update or relink images by embedding the graphics into your InDesign file as PageMaker can. While this eliminates the need to keep track of separate files, this option limits the flexibility of being able to manipulate the separate files and can make your files very large.

To embed a file, select it in the Links palette and choose Embed in the palette's flyout menu. An Embed icon indicates an embedded file in the Links palette. Later, you can select the embedded file name and select Unembed command from the palette menu if you need to relink to the original image file (or if you lost the original and want to get the picture out again).

Maintaining Editable Vectors

While InDesign can place native Illustrator (.AI) files, you can also copy Illustrator objects directly into InDesign through dragging and dropping or copying and pasting. We generally don't recommend pasting in artwork because it becomes embedded in a way that doesn't show up in the Links palette and you can't unembed. However, there's a way to copy objects from Illustrator or Freehand so that the vectors remain fully editable in InDesign, which can be very useful at times.

If you are using Illustrator 9 or later, you must first set up Illustrator's preferences properly. In Adobe Illustrator, select the File Handling & Clipboard Preferences (the exact name depends on your Illustrator version). Turn on the AICB option in the Clipboard portion of the preferences to keep objects editable when copied from Illustrator into InDesign (AICB is the Adobe Illustrator Clipboard format).

When you copy and paste one or more objects from Illustrator into InDesign, they become InDesign objects, and they can usually be edited just as if they were created using InDesign drawing tools. The same thing goes for objects that are dragged from Illustrator into InDesign.

You can also copy InDesign frames that have a stroke or fill and paste them into Illustrator for editing. This cross-application operability can be very handy when creating special effects for your layout.

Graphics

29

Scaling Graphics Precisely

When you place a picture in InDesign, the program sees it as two objects: the frame and the graphic nested inside of it. If you choose the Selection tool, you can manipulate both at the same time. If you choose the Direct Selection tool, you can manipulate the frame *or* the content—the graphic itself. Fortunately, InDesign displays the graphic bounding box in a different color (the inverse of the current layer color). Unlike QuarkXPress and PageMaker, when you apply numeric scaling to a graphic, InDesign gives you access to both the frame and the graphic bounding box, in some cases each may have a different scaling value!

So, when you manipulate a picture in InDesign, *always pay attention to which tool is selected.* Select an image with the Direct Selection tool to adjust only the image, or select it with the Selection tool to adjust *both* the image and its frame together. If you want to change the frame but not its contents, first Option/Alt-click on the frame with the Direct Selection tool, or use the Selection tool and turn off the Scale Content option in the Transform or Control palette's flyout menu.

Scaling Images

There are several ways to scale images in InDesign.

Scaling with Fitting Commands

You can choose menu commands (or a context menu, or keyboard shortcuts) to center or fit the graphic to the frame or the frame to the graphic. Select the graphic frame with the Selection tool and choose among these commands from the Fitting submenu (under the Object or context menu):

- Choose Fit Content Proportionally to resize the image to the maximum size that will proportionally fit the frame.

- Choose the Fit Content to Frame option to scale the image to the frame size, allowing it to distort.

- Use the Fit Frame to Content option to resize the frame so that it is the same size as the imported image.

- Use the Center Content option to center the graphic in the frame.

Scaling With Key Commands

You can also use keyboard shortcuts to change the size of an imported graphic. Press Ctrl-. (period) to increase the size of a selected image or press Command-,/Ctrl-, (comma) to reduce the size of an image. In either case you are adjusting the size in one percent increments. You can increase or decrease the size in five percent increments by adding the Option/Alt key. Note that the Ctrl-. shortcut only works in Windows.

Scaling with the Transform or Control Palette

After selecting an image, you can use the Transform or Control palette, the Scale tool, or the Free Transform tool to scale an image to a specific value (we discuss these methods in Chapter 10). If you use the Transform or Control palette, you can enter the percent to scale vertically or horizontally. If you want the horizontal and vertical values to be the same, click the "link" icon, then type one value and its value will be duplicated in the other field. Also, you can use these palettes to determine the scaling previously applied to an imported image, but be certain to click on the image with the Direct Selection tool to obtain an accurate reading of its scaling.

Scaling a Graphic by Dragging

You can also scale graphics interactively (but not precisely) by dragging the bounding box handles with the Selection tool as we describe in Chapter 10. To scale a graphic frame and its contents together, hold down the Command/Ctrl and Shift keys while dragging. Note that when you use this method, the frame doesn't retain the scaling value (the scale fields in the Transform or Control palette return to 100 percent). If you select the image with the Direct Selection tool, however, you can see the true scaling value.

Graphics

30

Display Options

One of the great technologies that Adobe has put under InDesign's hood is its ability to display graphics based upon their high-resolution information. This is a major step forward and provides you with a better representation on screen of what your printed piece will actually look like.

View Menu Settings

InDesign offers the ability to display each open document window with a different display setting. To change the setting, choose from the Display Performance submenu (in the View menu): Optimized Display, Typical Display, or High Quality Display (see Figure 30-1).

- **Optimized.** Select the Optimized setting (or press Command-Option-O/ Ctrl-Alt-O) to gray out all images and turn off transparency effects—useful when proofing or entering copy in long documents.

- **Typical.** You can choose this setting (or press Command-Option-Z/ Ctrl-Alt-Z) to view images with low-resolution proxy previews similar to the way they are displayed in QuarkXPress or PageMaker.

- **High Quality.** When you choose this setting (or press Command-Option-H/Ctrl-Alt-H) you can see your images at the same resolution they display in Photoshop and Illustrator. This is more or less "Display PostScript."

You might think that higher quality is always better. However, the High Quality display setting is calculation intensive and will slow down all but the fastest computers. If working in High Quality mode works for you, then go for it. But if you find InDesign displaying your pages very slowly, try using Typical or Optimized, or only applying the High Quality display mode to images that really need it (see below).

Individual Image Display Settings

InDesign lets you apply a display choice to each image via the Display Performance submenu in either the Object menu or the context menu. For instance, we often use Typical display for the document and then apply High Quality display on vector EPS images (which are notoriously difficult to see on screen).

If you have applied local display settings but then want to override them, choose Ignore Local Display Settings from the View menu. You can also remove an image's local display setting by selecting Use View Setting from the Display Performance submenu.

Setting Display Defaults

The three display settings are generally all you need, but InDesign lets you tweak them in the Display Performance panel of the Preferences dialog box. For example, we often change the text greeking to a smaller value because we'd rather look at tiny text than greeked, gray bars. If you really care about what all these settings do, check out David's book *Real World InDesign*.

Graphics

Figure 30-1
Display Quality

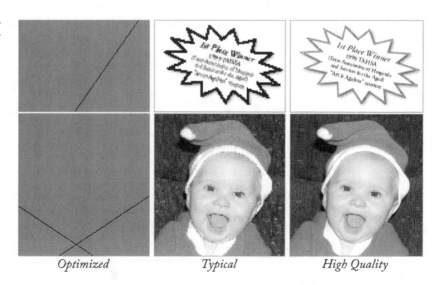

Optimized   *Typical*   *High Quality*

31

Clipping Paths

Clipping paths are PostScript (Bézier) paths that clip out a portion of an image. Clipping paths have long been the primary way to create "transparency" effects in PageMaker and QuarkXPress, but there are two problems with clipping paths. First, they can take a long time to draw. Second, they always have very sharp edges (part of the image is either in the path or outside of it). Because InDesign can now read image transparency (even soft-edged transparency), you may not have to or want to take the time to draw a clipping path.

Nevertheless, you may still need to deal with a clipping path from time to time, so we'd better explain how InDesign handles them. In short, InDesign deals with clipping paths almost exactly the way XPress and PageMaker do. (Of course, InDesign also adds a few fun options, too.)

Using Embedded Paths

Paths or clipping paths that you have saved within images in the TIFF, PSD or JPEG formats and imported into InDesign can be used to silhouette images. (Clipping paths in EPS files are *always* used.) You can apply a clipping path by selecting an image with the Selection or Direct Selection tool and choosing Clipping Path from the Object menu (or press Command-Option-Shift-K/Ctrl-Alt-Shift-K). Then, in the Clipping Path dialog box, select Photoshop Path from the Type popup menu. If there's more than one path embedded, choose which one you want to use (see Figure 31-1).

Figure 31-1
The Clipping Path
dialog box

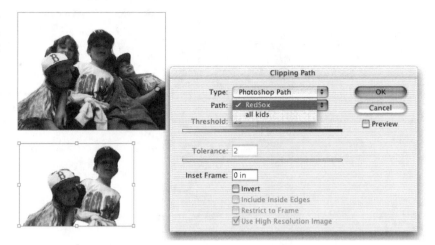

Creating Clipping Paths

If you import an image without an embedded clipping path, you can ask InDesign to create one using the Detect Edges option, which is similar to QuarkXPress's Non-white Areas clipping path feature. You can use this feature to drop out a solid colored (white or near-white) background behind an image. After selecting an image to clip and choosing the Clipping Path command from the Object menu, choose the Detect Edges option from the Type popup menu in the Clipping Path dialog box.

With the Detect Edges option selected, you can determine how close to the color white a pixel must be before it is ignored and removed from the visible area with the Threshold control (see Figure 31-2). Lighter backgrounds require a lower threshold whereas darker images require a higher value. The Tolerance setting determines how different a pixel is from the Threshold value for it to be recognized in creating the clipping path. Finally, the Inset Clipping Path choice lets you shrink the resulting clipping path, often to remove a white fringe around the image.

If the image has an extra channel in it, you can also tell InDesign to base the clipping path on it by choosing Alpha Channel from the Type popup menu in the Clipping Path dialog box. In this case, anything 50-percent black or darker in the channel is outside of the path.

In general, we usually shy away from using either the Detect Edges or the Alpha Channel features except perhaps for a quick comp. The results are just too clunky.

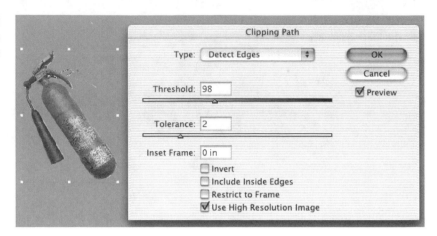

Figure 31-2
Clipping path made
with Detect Edges

Editing a Clipping Path

InDesign allows you to edit a clipping path which is imported or created. You might do this occasionally, for example, to perform a "quick fix" on a poorly created clipping path. In InDesign, in the anchor points of the clipping path appear whenever you select the image with the Direct Selection tool. You can then use any of the path-editing tools to edit a clipping path. If you open the Clipping Paths dialog box now, you'll see the Type popup menu has changed to User-Modified Path.

Converting Clipping Paths to Frames

Every so often, you need to convert a clipping path into an actual shape on the page. For example, you might want to place text on a path around an image in the same shape as the clipping path. This is simply impossible in PageMaker or QuarkXPress. However, you can do it easily in InDesign: Just right-click (or Control-click on the Mac) on the image to open the context menu, from which you can select Convert Clipping Path to Frame. InDesign replaces the image's frame with a new frame in the shape of the clipping path.

PART 8

Where Text Meets Graphics

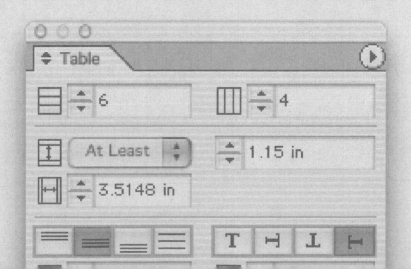

32

Inline Objects

What QuarkXPress calls anchored boxes, InDesign and PageMaker name *inline objects*. This chapter is where we talk about how you can anchor objects in text, so they flow when the text changes.

InDesign allows you to include text frames, graphics frames, frames without content, paths, text paths, and groups as inline objects. If you want to anchor multiple objects in the same place, you need to group them first. However, you can't link text in an inline object to another text frame.

Creating Inline Objects

There are two ways you can create inline objects in InDesign:

- You can use the XPress method: Select the object with the Selection tool and copy or cut it to the Clipboard. Then use the Type tool to click an insertion point where you want the object to be anchored, and use the Paste command under the Edit menu.

- You can use the PageMaker method: You can click an insertion point with the Type tool and choose Place from the File menu. Select a graphic file, and click Open. (Choosing a text file just inserts the text into the text flow in the original frame.)

We usually find the first method is more practical because you can size your inline object more easily before pasting.

Manipulating an Inline Object

Once an object is inline, it's treated like a character in the text flow, exactly as in XPress and PageMaker. You can drag an inline object up or down, but you can't drag it left or right because it's embedded in the text: You'll need to select it with the Type tool, and then cut and paste it to another position. (It's easy to select an inline object in the Story Editor because it displays as an icon in the text.) You can also click on it with the Selection tool before cutting, then paste it someplace else with the Type tool. To delete the object, select it—either click on it with the Selection tool or drag over it with the Type tool—and press the Delete key.

You can transform an anchored object in a variety of ways. You can use the Selection tool to drag the handles of a frame to change its size. You can extend the boundaries of the inline object past the right edge of the text frame, and you can apply transformations on an inline object with the Scale, Rotate, Shear, or Free Transform tools, or the Transform or Control palette. You can change the object's color or transparency. There are almost no limitations on these kinds of manipulations.

Adjusting Leading and Spacing

The object you paste or place inline must fit within the height of the text frame, though it can be wider. When you insert an inline object, you will probably have to adjust the space around it within the text. Here are some tips for doing that.

- If you want the object to sit between paragraphs of text, place it in a paragraph of its own. Select the object as we describe above, and set the leading to Auto in the Control or Character palette so the leading can expand, and it won't overlap the previous line. You can also adjust the paragraph Space Above or Space Below values.

- If you want the object to float within a line of text (for example, an icon graphic to be used in a manual), reduce its size with the Selection tool to fit inside the leading.

- To adjust the position of the inline object vertically, you can drag it up or down with the Selection or Direct Selection tool. However, we prefer to select the object with the Type tool, and adjust its position with Baseline Shift on the Character or Control palette because it's more accurate.

- To adjust the object's position horizontally, place an insertion point before or after the frame and adjust the Kerning value.

33

Text Wrap

When text meets graphics, or any two objects on your page overlap, your page layout application lets you choose how the two shall meet. In QuarkXPress, this choice is called runaround, and it's controlled in the Runaround panel of the Modify dialog box. In InDesign and PageMaker, it's called *text wrap*, and in InDesign, you make your choices in the Text Wrap palette.

Wrap Options

When you want to set the text wrap around an object, open the Text Wrap palette from the Type & Tables submenu in the Window menu (or press Command-Option-W/Ctrl-Alt-W) If necessary, choose Show Options from the palette's flyout menu to see the contour options at the bottom of the palette (see Figure 33-1).

InDesign lets you set the text wrap for almost any object—graphic frame, text frame, path, text path, or contentless frame. You cannot set the text wrap of an inline object, however. To set a default runaround, you set your default options on the Text Wrap palette with no object selected.

InDesign gives you five choices. The first three—No Text Wrap, Wrap Around Bounding Box, and Wrap Around Object Shape—correspond to the XPress options for runarounds. In addition, like in PageMaker, you can choose the Jump Object option (which forces text in any column touching the text wrap boundary to skip past the object), or Jump to Next Column (which forces text into the next column or text frame when it encounters a text wrap).

Figure 33-1
The Text Wrap
palette

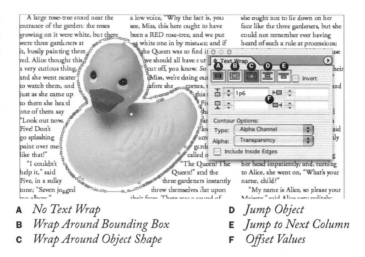

A *No Text Wrap*

B *Wrap Around Bounding Box*

C *Wrap Around Object Shape*

D *Jump Object*

E *Jump to Next Column*

F *Offset Values*

To create a text wrap in InDesign, select the object you want to wrap text around with the Selection or Direct Selection tool, and click one of the buttons in the palette. When you choose a rectangular wrap, you have the opportunity to set offset values on four sides of the object.

Creating Contours

InDesign provide several ways to create contours that follow the shape of a frame, the graphic inside a frame, a path, and so on. In InDesign, when you choose Wrap Around Object Shape, the contour options at the bottom of the palette become available.

Contour Choices

InDesign can read paths and clipping paths which are stored in TIFF, JPEG, EPS, and Photoshop PSD files. Select Photoshop Path from the Type popup menu in the Text Wrap palette, and then select the name of the path you want to use for the wrap in the Path menu. Similarly, if the image has an extra channel, you can use it by choosing Alpha, and then selecting the name of the channel to use.

There are other contour options as well: Graphic Frame follows the shape of the frame the graphic is in. Same as Clipping follows a clipping path saved with the graphic. Detect Edges uses InDesign's automatic edge detection, which only really works with graphics where there is a distinct edge to detect (when the image is against a white background).

To let text appear on the inside of an object, turn on the Include Inside Edges checkbox on the Text Wrap palette. To run text on the inside of an object rather than the outside, choose the Invert option.

Editing the Contour

InDesign displays the runaround path in a tint of the layer color whenever you select the graphic with the Direct Selection tool. Then you can use the Direct Selection tool and any of the path editing tools to edit the path (see Chapter 8).

Controlling Text Wrap

In QuarkXPress, runaround can only be applied when the text is below the runaround object (in the stacking order). In InDesign, by default, text wrap operates whether the wrap object is above or below the text. This can really mess up a new user, as text starts disappearing for "no reason." To change this behavior, turn on Text Wrap Only Affects Text Beneath in the Composition Preferences.

When you need to prevent text from wrapping around an object with a text wrap, select the text frame, choose Text Frame Options from the Object menu (or press Command-B/Ctrl-B), and turn on the Ignore Text Wrap option.

When you have text on more than one layer, you should also be aware of a Layer palette option that affects text wrap. When text wrap is turned on, by default it affects text even when the "wrap object" is on a hidden layer. To change that behavior, select Suppress Text Wrap When Layer Is Hidden in the Layer Options for the layer where the "wrap object" is located.

Where Text Meets Graphics

34

Text and Graphics on a Path

InDesign lets you set text along a path, as you can in QuarkXPress and illustration programs.

Creating Path Type

InDesign's text on a path works a bit differently than that in XPress. It doesn't use specialized tools to create the path: Instead, you can use any of the path creation and editing tools which we describe in Chapter 8. You can place type along any path—even the edge of a frame (but not along compound paths).

When you want to change a regular path into a text path, choose the Path Type tool, normally hidden under the Type tool (or press Shift-T). Then move the cursor over the path until you see a small + cursor. This indicates that if you click, or if you click and drag, you'll turn an ordinary path into a path type text frame.

If you click with the Path Type tool on an open path, an insertion point appears at the start of the path by default. (If the current default paragraph settings are not flush left or if they include an indent, the cursor may appear somewhere else on the path.) When you type or paste text, the text can extend the full length of the path. If you click on a closed path (like an oval), InDesign places the insertion point exactly where you clicked.

If you click and drag with the Path Type tool along the path instead, you determine where the text begins and ends on the path. Where you start dragging, a *start handle* appears, and as you're dragging an *end handle* moves along the path, indicating the end of the text (see Figure 34-1). After dragging to indicate where the text will go, type or paste text on the path.

At the center of the path text, a small vertical *center handle* also appears. In addition, because path type works like a single-line text frame, you also see an in port and out port which can be used for threading the text to or from another text path or a regular text frame.

Path Type Controls

InDesign offers several options for styling text in the Path Type Options dialog box, which you may open in one of three ways. The easiest method is to double-click the Path Type tool. You can also select Options from the Type on a Path submenu (under the Type menu), or you can use the context menu when path type is selected.

InDesign provides five path type effects (see Figure 34-2):

- **Rainbow.** This is the default style, in which characters follow the path, rotating along the curve.

- **Skew.** This effect rotates the characters along the curve, then skews them so they remains upright.

- **3D Ribbon.** This skews the characters, but doesn't rotate them.

- **Stair Step.** Here, the characters are neither rotated nor skewed.

- **Gravity.** This strange effect keeps the bottom of the characters' baseline on the path while keeping each vertical edge in line with the path's center point.

You can align the text to the path based on the text's baseline, center, ascender or descender. You can also adjust to the path's top, center or bottom. There is a Flip checkbox which allows you to flip the type you've created across the path. (You can also use the Selection or Direct Selection tool to drag the center handle of path type across the path to flip it.)

Where Text Meets Graphics

Figure 34-1
Watch the cursor change when you're working with path type text.

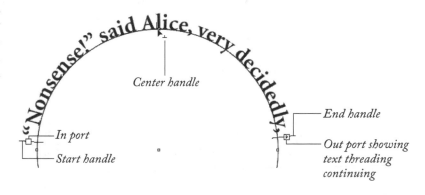

Center handle

End handle

In port

Out port showing text threading continuing

Start handle

Off with her head!   *Rainbow*

Off with her head!   *Skew*

Off with her head!   *3D Ribbon*

Off with her head!   *Stair Step*

Off with her head!   *Gravity*

The Spacing control lets you compensate for the fact that characters spread out when they are over a tight curve. By entering a positive value, InDesign removes extra space from characters near a curve, but leaves the spacing of those on straight segments unchanged.

Editing Path Type

You can use the Selection or Direct Selection tools to drag the path type handles, manipulating the position of the type along the path. (Be careful not to click the in port or out port.) You can also drag the center handle to finesse the positioning.

Threading Text

If not all your text fits on the path type frame, it gets overset. However, because path type has in and out ports, you can continue the text flow using InDesign's threading methods to create connections from one path to another, or between paths and regular text frames. Just use the Selection tool to click the in and out ports using the techniques we describe in Chapter 20.

Deleting Path Type

If you want to remove type from a path, select Delete Type from Path from the Type on a Path submenu (under the Type menu). This turns the path type "frame" into a regular path. If the path text is threaded, it will flow to another frame; if it is not, the text is deleted.

35

Creating and Importing Tables

Tables have been used as a visual way to communicate structured information for hundreds of years. While commands for creating and editing tables have long been available in word processing software and applications which work with structured documents like Adobe FrameMaker, Quark-XPress and InDesign have added table support only relatively recently. Tables are a relatively deep issue so our discussion will continue over the next two chapters.

Table Terminology

Before we describe how to create a table, we should discuss what a table is and how it differs from tabular material. A table is a grid of *cells,* arranged in horizontal *rows,* and vertical *columns* (see Figure 35-1). InDesign only has text cells, but allows table cells to contain inline graphics.

Tables have their own specialized terminology, so it's worth taking a moment to be clear what the different parts of a table are called. The line which may surround a table is called the table's *border.* Each cell has a *fill*, and it is surrounded by *strokes.* InDesign lets you set the fill or stroke to None (transparent), a color, or a gradient. InDesign even lets you set the stroke attributes on each side of the cell individually. You can define *header rows* and *footer rows* which can be repeated when the table flows into another frame or page.

Figure 35-1
Tables are grids
of cells.

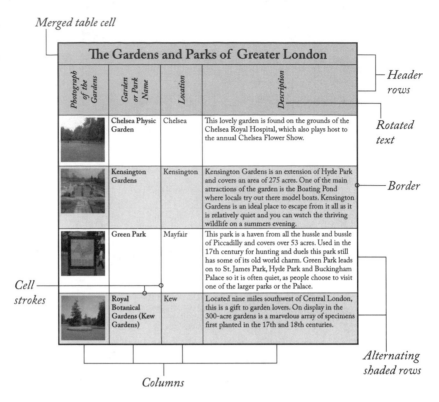

Merged table cell

Header rows

Rotated text

Border

Cell strokes

Alternating shaded rows

Columns

Tables versus Tabs

Desktop publishers have long used tabs to create simple tables (see Chapter 23). However, tables—especially as they're are implemented in InDesign—are much more powerful. Here are some reasons to use tables.

- You can have multiple lines of text in a single cell, which is impossible with tabs.

- Adding background colors and rules is much easier with tables.

- Alignment and spacing can be set very precisely inside and outside of InDesign tables.

- Editing a table is much easier than editing tabular material. You can easily select cells, rows, columns or the entire table to make changes quickly.

Creating a New Table

For InDesign, a table is always an inline (anchored) object in a text frame. To create a new table, place a text insertion point in a frame and choose

Insert Table from the Table menu (or press Command-Option-Shift-T/ Ctrl-Alt-Shift-T). In the Insert Table dialog box, you define the initial structure of the table—the number of rows high, and columns wide, and the number of header and footer rows. When you click OK, InDesign creates a table the width of the enclosing text frame.

You can also convert text which contains tab and return characters (a tabular structure) into a table. First, turn on Show Hidden Characters in the Type menu and make sure that there are tab characters where you want columns to be formed, and return characters at the end of each line where you want a row to be defined. Then select the text, and choose Convert Text to Table from the Table menu.

Entering Text in a Table

To enter text into your table, use the Type tool to place a text insertion point in a cell and start typing. You can press the Tab key to advance from cell to cell. (If you press Tab in the last cell, a new row will be created.) Press Shift-Tab to move to the previous cell. Press Return to add a paragraph return within a cell. As you add text (unless you have defined the cell to be a fixed size) the cell expands vertically, but not horizontally. You can also use the Left, Right, Up, and Down Arrow keys to move between cells.

Importing Tables

InDesign also allows you to import tables created in Microsoft Word and spreadsheets created in Microsoft Excel—just place the file as you would any other text file. You can also copy and paste from Word and Excel documents.

When importing a table, you can choose whether or not to retain the original formatting in the Import Options available when you choose Place from the File menu. However, you can always reformat it in InDesign using the methods we describe in the following chapters.

Converting Tables to Text

It's also possible to convert a table to tabbed text. When InDesign does this, it adds tab characters between each column, and return characters at the end of each row. The best reason to do this might be to create tab-delimited text which can be imported back into a spreadsheet application.

Where Text Meets Graphics

36

Formatting Tables

Once you've created or imported a table, it's time to begin formatting it. In this chapter, we begin by discussing how to select tables and parts of tables. We then discuss the tools for formatting tables—the commands under the Table menu, the Table palette and other palettes and context menus. We cover how to change a table's structure—its size, the rows and columns that make it up, and the strokes and fills of the individual cells. Finally, we discuss table alignment and spacing.

Selecting Tables

To format a table, you need to know how to select it and its elements. As we discussed in the previous chapter, tables are always contained within a text frame. To perform any selection, you must start by choosing the Type tool.

Selecting Cells

If you want to select a single cell, click an insertion point or select text with the Type tool, then choose Cell from the Select submenu (under the Table menu or from the context menu). Or, faster, just press the Escape (Esc) key.

You can select multiple cells by clicking in a cell and dragging horizontally, vertically, or diagonally. Another method to select several cells is to select a single cell and then press the Shift key with the Up, Down, Left or Right Arrow keys to extend the selection.

Selecting Rows or Columns

When you want to select rows or columns, you can also use either menu commands or the mouse. The slow way: select text in the row or column you want to select, then choose Row or Column from the Select submenu (under the Table menu or context menu). The fast way: If you want to select a row, move your cursor along the left edge of the row until you see the right-pointing arrow cursor (see Figure 36-1). Click to select the row. Dragging upward or downward extends the selection to other rows.

Selecting columns with the mouse is just as easy. To select a column, move your cursor along the top edge of the column until you see a down-pointing arrow cursor, then click (or drag).

Selecting the Entire Table

There are three ways to select every cell in a table: First, you can place the text cursor in the table and then choose Table from the Select submenu (in the Table menu or context menu). Or, you can also move your cursor to the upper-left corner of the table and when you see the diagonal arrow cursor, click to select the table. Or, even better, you can simply press a shortcut: Command-Option-A/Ctrl-Alt-A.

Tools for Table Formatting

You can find almost every table-related feature in the Table menu, and most table-formatting features in the Table Options dialog box (press Command-Option-T/Ctrl-Alt-T).

There is also the Cell Options dialog box (press Command-Option-B/Ctrl-Alt-B, where you can set the attributes of selected cells. These include text attributes that we talk about in the next chapter; the stroke and fill attributes; row height, column width, and keep options (we also

Figure 36-1
Move along the left side of the table. When you see the right-pointing arrow click to select the row.

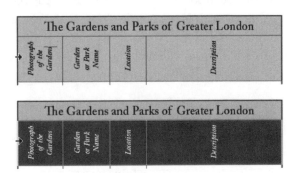

discuss the latter in the next chapter); and diagonal lines which can be applied across a cell.

InDesign also has a Table palette which contains the most common formatting options. If it's not open, choose Table from the Window menu. However, we usually choose table commands from either a context menu, or in the Control palette. If you have at least one cell selected, the Control palette shows the most common table controls.

Editing a Table's Structure

Tables almost never spring into being perfectly; you'll likely need to change the overall size of the table or of the rows and columns, add or delete rows or columns, merge two or more cells into one, or split a cell into smaller cells. It's all possible, and it's all easy.

Scaling the Entire Table

InDesign allows you to scale an entire table by dragging. First, click anywhere in the table with the Type tool, and move the cursor over the lower-right corner of the table. When you see the diagonal double-headed arrow cursor (see Figure 36-2), drag to scale the table. Holding down the Shift key constrains the scaling proportionally. (You can't scale a table if the table spans more than one text frame.)

Adding Rows and Columns

There are several ways to add rows or columns to a table. First, you can use the Insert dialog box: Place the text cursor in a row or column next to where you want the new row or column to appear. Next, choose either Row or Column from the Insert submenu (in the Table menu or from the context menu). Then enter the number of rows or columns and whether you want them above, below, to the left, or the right of the current cell.

You can also add rows by dragging: Position the Type tool over a row or column boundary until you see the double-headed arrow cursor (see Figure 36-2). Hold down the mouse button, and then press the Option/Alt key while dragging downward (for rows) or to the right (for columns).

Figure 36-2
Cursors for scaling the table and dragging cell or row boundaries

Scale table cursor

Drag row boundary cursor

Drag column boundary cursor

Finally, you can use the Table Options dialog box or the Control or Table palette to add rows or columns. Increasing the number of rows or columns in the dialog box or the palette adds rows at the bottom of the table, or columns on the right side of the table.

Deleting Rows, Columns, and Entire Tables

You have similar flexibility when deleting rows and columns. Using the Type tool, you can click in a cell (or select multiple cells) and then choose Row or Column from the Delete submenu (under the Table menu or the context menu). You can also use the dragging method to delete cells on the right or bottom side of the table: Position the Type tool over the bottom or right side of the table until you see the double-headed arrow cursor. Hold down the mouse, then press the Option/Alt key. If you drag upward or to the left, rows or columns are deleted.

If you want to delete the entire table, when there is an insertion point or a selection, choose Table from the Delete submenu (under the Table menu or context menu).

Merging, Unmerging, and Splitting Cells

You can merge together cells in the same row or column by selecting them, then choosing Merge Cells from the Table menu (or context menu). If there is content in the cells, InDesign combines it into one cell. Once merged, you select the Unmerge Cells command to restore their previous condition.

To split a cell into two smaller cells, use the Type tool to click inside the cell and then choose Split Cell Horizontally or Split Cell Vertically from the Table menu (or context menu).

Changing Row or Column Size

You can change a table's row or column size by dragging or numerically. If you like working interactively, just click and drag a row or column boundary (you'll see the double-headed arrow cursor if you're in the right place). Note that this changes your table's width or height; in fact, you can extend it beyond the right edge of the text frame. If you want to change a row or column boundary without resizing the whole table, hold down the Shift key while you drag. You can also resize all the rows or columns proportionately by holding down the Shift key while dragging the right edge (for rows) or bottom edge (for columns) of the table.

To change row width or column height numerically, first select the rows or columns to be resized (or just place the text cursor in any cell in

Where Text Meets Graphics

the row or column). Then you can choose Rows and Columns from the Cell Options submenu (under the Table menu or context menu). Similarly, you can change the values in the Row Height and Column Width fields of the Control or Table palette.

When you don't know exactly how high a row should be, choose At Least from the popup menu next to the Row Height field. This sets a minimum row height that autoexpands as text or graphics are added to the cells in the row. Alternatively, you can use the Exactly option to set the row height to be a particular value.

One last trick: You can give selected rows or columns the same height or width by selecting the rows or columns you want to change, and choosing Distribute Rows Evenly or Distribute Columns Evenly from the Table or context menu.

Setting Strokes and Fills

You can set the fill and stroke attributes for the table as a whole, or for individual cells. The colors available are those which have been created in the Swatches palette, including None. You can choose any stroke style for cell strokes, and you can set stroke color (and gap color, if necessary).

The line which surrounds the table is called the *border*. To set the border attributes, choose Table Options from the Table menu. In the Table Border section of the dialog box, you can set the border's line weight, color, line type, and overprinting attribute.

Fill and Stroke Options

To set the fills and strokes for table cells with the Cell Options dialog box, select the cells you want to affect, choose Cell Options from the Table menu, and click on the Strokes and Fills panel. Here you can set the characteristics for the strokes of the selected table or cells: their weight, color, line type, gap color, and overprinting attributes. In the same dialog, you can set the fill color and overprinting characteristics.

When setting stroke attributes, use the proxy image to select which segments you want to apply the change to (see Figure 36-3). Click the segments to select and deselect them—selected segments are blue, deselected segments are gray. For example, to change the outside strokes of the selected cells, click on the inside segments to deselect them. Alternatively, you can set stroke attributes of cells using the Control or Stroke palettes. You can set fill attributes in the Swatches palette.

Adding Diagonal Lines

You can also apply diagonal lines to cells. Select the cells you want to affect, and choose Diagonal Lines from the Cell Options submenu (under the Table menu). In the Diagonal Lines panel, you can select the type of diagonal line you want, and whether it prints in front of or behind the contents of the cell. You can also choose the line's weight, line type, color, gap color, and overprinting attributes.

Headers and Footers

You can create headers and footers which are formatted differently than the body of the table. Often you want these special rows to be repeated automatically when a table continues into a different frame, or onto a different page. The controls for creating these are found in the Headers and Footers panel of the Table Options dialog box. Here you can specify how many headers and footers are in the table, and how frequently they repeat. You can also convert body rows to header or footer rows from the Table or context menus.

Creating Alternating Patterns

It's often helpful to apply an alternating pattern of strokes or fills to the cells of a table to make it more readable or to improve its appearance. InDesign lets you create these alternating patterns automatically. That means that as you subsequently edit the table, adding or deleting rows and columns, the pattern remains true.

Figure 36-3
The stroke proxy in the Cell Options dialog box

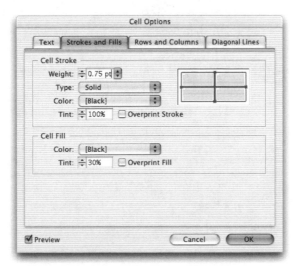

Where Text Meets Graphics

Adding Alternate Fills or Strokes

To create alternating fills in your table, click anywhere in the table and choose Table Options from the Table menu. Then, in the Alternating Fills panel, choose an alternating pattern: every other row, every second or third row, or whatever. You may wish to skip a certain number rows at the top or bottom of the table. Similarly, you can specify alternating row or column strokes in the Alternating Row Strokes or Alternating Column Strokes panels of the Table Options dialog box.

Alignment and Spacing Within a Cell

Each cell is like a miniature text frame, and it's not surprising that the options for alignment and spacing are very similar to those of text frames. The Text panel of the Cell Options dialog box is the equivalent of the Text Frame Options dialog box, and it mainly affects vertical alignment within the cell. In addition, you can use the controls on the Paragraph palette to control horizontal alignment, indents, and the spacing between paragraphs inside a cell. You can also set some of these options, such as Cell Inset, in the Table palette.

Alignment and Spacing Around a Table

A table always sits inside of a text frame, so you must also consider its relationship to that frame. Here are how some ways you can do that.

- **Horizontal Alignment.** The table may not fill the width of the text frame. If that is so, then you can click an insertion point to the right or left of the table (the blinking insertion point should appear as tall as the table). Then use the Paragraph palette horizontal alignment controls to set how the table aligns to the frame.

- **Space Before and After.** You can set the space above and below a table using the Space Before and Space After fields in the Paragraph palette, but you have to put the cursor in the same paragraph as the table (not inside the table). Or, put the cursor inside the table and choose Table Setup from the Table Options submenu (under the Table menu). In the Table Spacing section of the dialog box, you can set the space before and after values. Space Before doesn't apply when the table is at the top of a frame.

37

Text and Graphics in Tables

Now that you know how to format the table itself, it's time to talk about formatting text and graphics *inside* table cells.

Text Formatting

Text inside a table cell acts almost exactly like text inside any text frame, and you can format it to your heart's delight. If you need to format a bunch of cells in the same way, select them all before applying the attributes. You can even delete all the text from all selected cells by pressing the Delete key. Note that you can format table cells even with no text in them. That way, the text in each cell gets formatted automatically later, as you type.

Tabs within Tables

Ordinarily you wouldn't type a tab character inside a table cell, but if you need one—to align decimal numbers within a cell, for example—you can add one by either using the Insert Special Character submenu (see Chapter 22) or by typing Option-Tab on the Macintosh. Alt-Tab switches applications in Windows, so set up your own keyboard shortcut.

Overset Text in a Cell

By default, cells automatically expand vertically when you add text or graphics. However, if you've set rows to have a fixed height, when you add text or graphics beyond that size, you may see a small red dot appear in the lower right corner of the cell. This indicates overset text. You can either make the cell bigger or make the cell's contents smaller.

Text Rotation

Unlike XPress, which allows any arbitrary text angle inside a cell, InDesign allows text to be rotated in multiples of 90 degrees. To rotate text, select the cell or cells you want to affect and click on one of the text rotation buttons in the Control or Table palette. You can also use the Text panel of the Cell Options dialog box.

Table Flow Between Text Frames

If you have a long table, you can flow it from one text frame another. Each row acts like a line of text, so the table always breaks between rows; you can't break the table part way through a row.

Just as in working with paragraph text, you can use Keep Options to control where a row begins and whether it is kept with the next row. However, the Keep Options for tables are in the Rows and Columns panel of the Cell Options dialog box.

Pasting or Placing Graphics

In XPress, you can convert a table cell into a picture box. However, the only way to get a picture into an InDesign table cell is to insert it as an inline (anchored) object. Once pasted or placed, it can be manipulated like any inline object. (We discuss what inline objects are and how to work with them in Chapter 32.)

We've found that you'll get the most control over the process if you place your graphic on the page first and scale it to the approximate size of the cell *before* you paste it into a table cell. You should also consider setting the row height, cell alignment, and clipping options for the cell *before* placing the graphic.

Handling Overset Graphics

InDesign usually tries to let a graphic expand above and to the right of the cell, even if it doesn't fit. But you may sometimes see an overset condition when you paste or place graphics into a table cell. This is because the object being placed exceeds the space available for it. Our experience is that this most often happens with graphics when the Text Inset values are too large, or when you make the cell height smaller than the First Baseline Offset value. You can also select the cell and adjust the Text Inset or First Baseline Offset values to get the graphic to fit.

PART 9

Color and Transparency

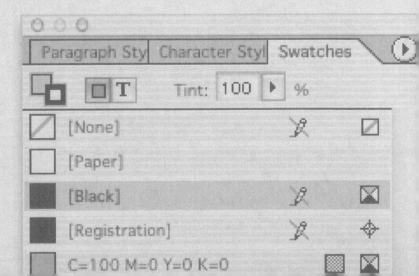

38

Creating and Applying Colors

InDesign uses two different palettes to create and manipulate colors. One of them, the Swatches palette, follows the PageMaker and QuarkXPress model of working with named colors. The other is the Color palette—similar to the Color palette in Adobe Illustrator and Photoshop—which allows you to use sliders to mix colors, and which can create and apply colors without naming them. You can mix colors in InDesign in CMYK, RGB, and Lab (but not HSB or HLS) color models, and you can define colors as either process or spot.

Swatches Palette

We recommend that you use the Swatches palette to create and edit your colors. The advantage of creating named colors here is that—as in QuarkXPress and PageMaker—it makes it easier for you or your service provider to globally change the colors in your document later on, should that be necessary.

If the Swatches palette is not open, choose the Swatches palette from the Window menu, or press F5 (see Figure 38-1). The palette lists all the colors currently in your document, along with icons indicating the color model and whether the color is spot or process. There are controls for applying color to fills and strokes, and creating tints and gradients.

There are four built-in swatches which always appear in the Swatches palette and which can't be removed: None, Black, Registration, and Paper; the last, Paper, simulates the paper color on which you're printing. InDesign also includes swatches for cyan, yellow, magenta, red, green, and blue.

Figure 38-1

The Swatches palette

A *Fill/Stroke control*
B *Text/Object control*
C *Tint slider*
D *Color swatch*
E *Gradient swatch*
F *Tint swatch*
G *Spot color*
H *Process color*
I *RGB color*
J *CMYK color*
K *Show All Swatches button*
L *Show Colors button*
M *Show Gradients button*
N *New Swatch button*
O *Delete Swatch button*

However, red, green, and blue are defined as CMYK colors (unlike XPress and PageMaker) so it's OK to use them.

From the palette's flyout menu, you can choose to display just swatches by choosing Large Swatch, or you can display each swatch with its name by choosing Name. You can also display more swatches at a time by choosing either Small Swatches or Small Name from the palette menu. At the bottom of the palette, there are buttons to show all swatches, only color swatches, or only gradient swatches.

Creating Swatches

To create a new color, choose New Color Swatch from the palette's flyout menu. This opens the New Color Swatch dialog box (see Figure 38-2). A faster way of opening the dialog is to select any color other than None or Paper and then Option/Alt-click the New Swatch button on the palette. Here you can name your swatch, choose its color model, and specify whether the color is process or spot. When editing the color composition, you can either drag the sliders or type values. For process colors the default is to name colors by their color components, but if you turn off the Name with Color Value option, you can give a color any name.

If you add colors when you have no documents open, they'll be available for all future documents you create.

Tint Swatches

InDesign lets you create swatches that are tints (shades) of other swatches. For example, if you use 20-percent cyan behind every sidebar in your publication, make this a swatch to apply it quickly. Later, if you decide you want

Figure 38-2
The New Color
Swatch dialog box

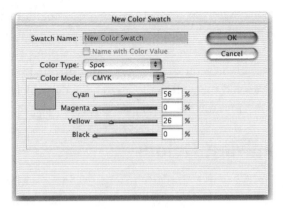

15-percent magenta instead, you can edit the swatch (by double-clicking on it) and all the tints will change throughout your document. To make a tint swatch, select a color in the palette and choose New Tint Swatch from the flyout menu.

Color Palette

The second option for creating new colors is the Color palette, which works more like creating colors in Illustrator or Photoshop (see Figure 38-3). If it's not open, choose the Color palette from the Window menu, or press F6, then choose a color mode (LAB, CMYK, or RGB) from the palette's flyout menu. You can pick a color either by moving the sliders, typing a value, or clicking in the color bar.

Saving Unnamed Colors

The Color palette is nice if you like working interactively. However, we don't like it for two reasons. First, it's too easy to get fooled into trusting the color you see on screen instead of picking colors from a printed swatch book. You cannot trust what you see on screen unless you have spent time setting up the color management system. Second, these colors are not automatically saved in the Swatches palette for future use, and unnamed colors are a hassle for everyone, especially your output provider.

Figure 38-3
The Color palette

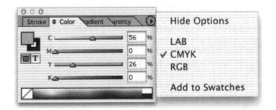

Color & Transparency

Fortunately, you can turn unnamed colors into named swatches by dragging the color proxy in the Color palette into the Swatches palette or by choosing Add to Swatches from the Color palette's flyout menu. Even better, if you've created a bunch of unnamed colors in your document you can add them all to the Swatches palette by choosing Add Unnamed Colors from the Swatches palette menu.

Applying Colors

InDesign works similarly to QuarkXPress when it comes to applying colors: Select one or more frames, and then select whether you want to change the fill or the stroke attributes. These choices are found in three places: on the bottom of the Tools palette, and on the upper left corner of the Swatches and Color palettes. You can also toggle between these two options by typing the letter X.

You can then click a swatch on the Swatches palette or choose a color from the Color palette. You can also apply colors by dragging a color swatch from these palettes onto the fill or stroke of a frame, even if the frame is not the selected object. If you pick the wrong attribute—fill instead of stroke, or *vice versa*—Shift-X swaps the fill and stroke colors.

Changing the Color of Type

When selecting a text frame with the Selection or Direct Select tool, you also need to tell InDesign whether you want to color the frame or the type inside the frame. There are two additional buttons found on the Tools, Swatches, and Color palettes: Formatting Affects Frame and Formatting Affects Text. It's crucial to pay attention to these because InDesign can apply a stroke color to text without converting the text to outlines. You can even apply a fill color of None to make the text transparent (though of course you'll probably want to give the text a stroke or something to make it visible in some other way).

Applying Color to Lines

Coloring lines (paths) works the same as applying color to frames. Just select the path's stroke or fill attribute, and then use the Swatches or Color palette to pick a color. Note that InDesign is very flexible because you can also apply color to the fill of an unclosed path. (Filled lines act just like closed paths; it's as though there were an invisible line from the end point to the beginning point of the line.)

Colorizing Images

QuarkXPress, PageMaker, and InDesign let you apply color to a grayscale or black-and-white (Bitmap) TIFF image. But when applying colors, you have to get accustomed to using the right tool to select the right item.

XPress and InDesign let you apply a color to the background of an image's frame to create a "fake-duotone effect." Apply the fill color with the Selection tool, then select the image with the Direct Select tool and turn on the Overprint Fill feature in the Attributes palette.

If you want to colorize the image itself (only grayscale or black-and-white TIFF, JPEG, or PSD files with no transparency), you must select it using the Direct Select tool. As we explain in Chapter 28, this selects the graphic, rather than the frame. Then you can use either the Swatches or Color palette to apply a color to the image.

Gradients

In QuarkXPress you can create *blends* which can be applied to the background of boxes. InDesign allows you to create *gradients* which are considerably more flexible.

Gradient Swatches

Creating gradients is similar to creating color swatches: Select New Gradient Swatch from the Swatches palette's flyout menu. In the New Gradient Swatch dialog box you can set the color and tint of each end separately by clicking on the little box (called a "stop") under the Gradient Ramp at the bottom of the dialog box (see Figure 38-4). Then you can either choose from colors listed in your Swatches palette (by selecting Swatches from the Stop Color popup menu), or mix a new color by choosing a color model such as CMYK. You can also choose between a Linear or Radial gradient from the Type popup menu.

You can add additional colors to your gradient by clicking just below the Gradient Ramp and selecting the color for the new stop. You can, of course, drag the stops around (even reversing the order of the blend by switching the two end stops) or move them by typing a percentage value in the Location field. To remove a stop, just drag it from the ramp. You can even move the midpoint between two stops by dragging the diamonds on top of the Gradient Ramp.

Gradients are applied to objects and text just like any solid color. Select the object you want to change and either select a gradient color on the Swatches palette, or drag the gradient to the object.

Color & Transparency

Figure 38-4
The New Gradient
Swatch dialog box

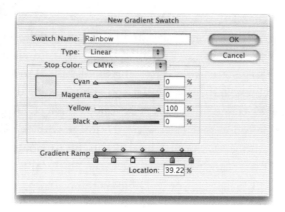

Gradient Palette

You can also create and edit gradients with the Gradient palette, which you can open from the Window menu (choose Show Options from the palette's flyout menu to see all its controls).

This palette is the equivalent of the Color palette—that is, it lets you create local, unnamed gradients on objects. Because we'd rather have named gradient swatches, we rarely use this palette to create blends. However, if you like working interactively like this, you can use this palette in a similar way to the New Gradient Swatch dialog box—clicking on color stops, editing colors using the Color palette, and so on. There are two features not available in the dialog box: You can reverse the colors in the gradient by clicking the reverse button, and you can change the angle of the gradient.

Gradient Tool

The Gradient tool lets you apply or edit a blend, controlling the direction and length of the gradient. First, select the object you wish to modify, then drag the Gradient tool across the object in the direction you wish the gradient to go. The distance you click and drag also controls the start and stop points of the gradient: Drag a short distance to create a gradient with an abrupt transition between colors or drag a greater distance to create a longer gradient. This, too, creates unnamed gradients that are hard to control later. It's a great tool, but we prefer to control gradients using swatches.

Eyedropper Tool

Simply put, the Eyedropper tool—found in InDesign's Tools palette but nowhere in XPress or PageMaker—is a cool tool to have in a page layout program. With it you can quickly copy all formatting attributes from an object and apply them to one or more objects, either selected or not.

Copying and Applying Colors

The Eyedropper tool lets you copy colors used in any open document, including those in placed bitmapped images. For example, if you wish to match the color of the type in a headline to the color of a car which appears in a placed picture, select the text with the Type tool and then click on the car with the Eyedropper tool. The Eyedropper immediately applies the color to any selected object, so you might consider pressing Command-Shift-A/Ctrl-Shift-A to deselect all objects before using it.

Eyedropper Tool Status

The Eyedropper tool is ready to pick up formatting when it is filled with white and facing down towards the left. Once you have clicked on something, the cursor changes—filled with black and facing down to the right—meaning its ready to apply formatting. If you've picked up text formatting with the Eyedropper tool, the cursor will also have an I-beam attached to it. If you choose an incorrect color or formatting, hold down the Option/Alt key and resample a different color with the Eyedropper tool.

As long as the cursor is filled with black, you can continue to apply formatting to other objects—selected or not—by clicking on them with the "filled" cursor.

The color you select with the Eyedropper tool appears in the Color palette. We highly recommend saving this color into the Swatches palette as a named color.

Eyedropper Options

You can choose which attributes you want to copy with the Eyedropper tool by double-clicking on the tool in the Tools palette. The Eyedropper Options dialog box has five different sets of settings for copying fill, stroke, transparency, character, and paragraph attributes. By default, all are turned on. Then, within each category you can select the exact choices you want to include by clicking in the checkboxes. For instance, you can tell InDesign to pick up the font, size, and color of text, but ignore its leading and tint.

Colors & Color Libraries

Color libraries are groups of colors that have been saved together, added to the Swatches palette, and used in your document. Popular color libraries

Color & Transparency

that ship with InDesign include Pantone, Trumatch, and Web-safe colors. Because libraries can contain thousands of colors each, InDesign does not automatically add them all to your Swatches palette; you must add colors one at a time.

You can access colors stored in libraries by choosing New Color Swatch from the Swatches palette's flyout menu and then selecting a library by name. InDesign's 16 color libraries are listed under the Color Mode popup menu following the RGB, CMYK and LAB color models.

To find a particular color in a library, either scroll through the list or type the color's number code. To add that color to your Swatches palette, click Add. Then either continue picking colors, or click OK.

Importing Colors

There are a number of other ways to add colors to your document besides adding them from a library. While InDesign does not have an Append feature like XPress, it does let you grab colors from other documents: In the New Color Swatch dialog box, you can choose Other Library from the Color Mode popup menu and select another InDesign document or an EPS file from Illustrator 8 or earlier (later versions of Illustrator won't work because they use a different format). Then, in the dialog box that next appears, select the colors to add as described above.

Of course, when you open a PageMaker or QuarkXPress document the colors are imported automatically. And when you import an EPS or Illustrator file, InDesign adds the graphic's spot colors (if there are any) to the Swatches palette. With an Illustrator file, it even including the named tints and gradients. Copying objects from one InDesign document to another copies any applied named swatches, too.

Editing and Deleting Colors

You can edit a color by selecting a color in the Swatches palette and choose Swatch Options from the palette menu. Even faster: simply double-click the swatch. Watch out: this applies the color to any selected objects on your page!

You can duplicate a swatch color (perhaps in order to edit it to make a similar color) by selecting a swatch and choosing Duplicate Swatch from the palette menu. But it's even faster just to click on the color and then click the New Color Swatch button at the bottom of the Swatches palette (or Option/Alt-click to duplicate and immediately edit it).

You can delete individual swatches by selecting one or more and either choosing Delete Swatch from the palette menu or dragging the swatches to the Delete Swatch button. InDesign asks you if you want to replace the color with another swatch; InDesign also gives you the option to leave the color alone (it becomes an unnamed color). If you want to delete all the unused colors in your document, first choose Select All Unused from the Swatches palette's flyout menu and then press the Delete Swatch button.

Deleting spot colors which come from EPS files can sometimes be tricky. If you delete the EPS file, the added spot colors appear to be locked. To remove them, Select All Unused from the menu, deselect any colors which should be retained, and then use the Delete Swatch command.

Converting Spot Colors to Process

You can convert spot colors from a library, such as Pantone colors, to process colors by editing the color (double-click on the color swatch) and then choosing CMYK from the Color Mode popup menu. You can also use the Ink Manager (which you can select in either the Swatches palette or the Print dialog box; see Chapter 43). Be aware that some Pantone colors don't have close CMYK equivalents.

Mixed Ink Swatches and Groups

What QuarkXPress calls Multi-ink colors—combinations of spot colors, or spot and process colors—InDesign calls *mixed ink swatches*. To use this feature, you need to have at least one spot color in your Swatches palette.

You can create a mixed ink swatch by choosing New Mixed Ink Swatch from the Swatches palette flyout menu. In the New Mixed Ink Swatch dialog box (see Figure 38-5), choose an ink, and enter a tint percentage of this color by either dragging the slider, or typing a value. Continue this process for one or more other colors. Then click Add to add the color to the Swatches palette, and either continue adding swatches or click OK.

Figure 38-5
Making mixed inks

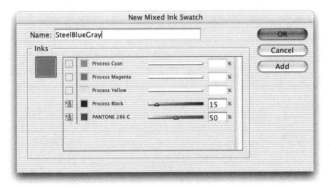

193

You can also create a group of mixed ink swatches which share colors using the New Mixed Ink Group command from the Swatches palette flyout menu. Mixed Ink Groups are useful when you need a number of different swatches based on varying tint builds of two or more colors. However, unfortunately, the interface is nonintuitive. See *Real World InDesign* for more on mixed ink groups and other in-depth spot color issues.

Note that when you create a mixed ink group, it also adds a "group" swatch to the Swatches palette. You can't apply this swatch to objects, but if you can double-click it to edit the group.

Setting Overprints

InDesign's overprinting controls are hiding in the Attributes palette (see Figure 38-6), which is available from the Window menu. Here you can set whether to overprint the fill, the stroke, or the gap of a selected object.

Figure 38-6

The Attributes palette

Previewing and Printing Overprints

While you can specify overprinting in XPress, there is no way to preview its effect (either on screen or on a non-PostScript color printer) before making color separations. In InDesign, you can: Select Overprint Preview from the View menu to see how overprinted inks will appear. You can work while this is turned on, but it does slow InDesign down a little bit. In addition, when printing composite color prints or making PDF files, you can turn on the Simulate Overprint option. The result is not suitable for final prepress work, but it excellent for inkjet printers and proofing.

39

Transparency

QuarkXPress and PageMaker exemplify page layout as it has been done for decades: opaque objects laid out next to each other or overlapping one another. If you want a non-rectangular edge around an image, you can create a clipping path in Photoshop. If you need soft edges, drop shadows, feathering, or any other sort of raster effect, you have to create it in Photoshop or with a third-party plug-in.

Adobe decided that this was silly, and added all kinds of cool transparency effects to InDesign. That's what we're going to talk about in this chapter. However, when it comes to printing transparency effects, we'll hold off until Chapter 44. (Suffice it to say for now that this stuff really does print. This is Adobe we're talking about here.)

Importing Transparent Objects

With InDesign you can import transparent graphics saved as native Photoshop (.PSD), Illustrator (.AI), or Acrobat 5 or 6 PDF documents (PDF 1.4 or later). For example, you can create a cloud with wispy, feathered edges in Photoshop (fading out to Photoshop's checkerboard transparency) and when you bring it into InDesign the soft edge is retained, revealing any InDesign objects under it (see Figure 39-1).

The most reliable file formats to use for transparent imported graphics are the newest ones: Photoshop 6 or later, Illustrator 10 or later, and PDF 1.4 or later. Photoshop 6 and later can also save TIFF files with transparency. However, if you flatten an image in Photoshop, you lose all transparency.

Figure 39-1
Transparent objects
from Photoshop
or Illustrator retain
their transparency in
InDesign.

In Photoshop

In InDesign

Applying Transparency

InDesign also lets you can make any page object—frames, lines, or imported graphics—transparent with the Transparency palette (under the Window menu or press Shift-F10). The two settings you can make here are Opacity and Blending Mode. To change a selected object's Opacity, choose an level of transparency by either entering a percentage or using the slider. The lower the value the more transparent the object becomes. Note that you can't change the opacity of individual characters in a text frame—it's all the text or nothing—so select text frames with the Selection tool to apply transparency.

Blending Modes

You can control how transparent objects blend with colors beneath them by choosing one of the blending modes within the Transparency palette. If you're familiar with Photoshop, you may already know these.

- **Normal.** At 100-percent opacity, the top color completely replaces the bottom color—that is, transparency is turned off.

- **Multiply.** Darkens the base color by multiplying its values with those of the blend color. This mode is usually the best choice for drop shadows.

- **Screen.** Lightens the color by multiplying the inverse of the blend and base colors, an effect similar to projecting two slides on the same screen.

- **Overlay.** Multiplies or screens the colors, depending on the base color, but tries to limit the effect so that highlights and shadows are preserved.

- **Soft Light.** Soft Light is like Overlay, but doesn't try to preserve highlight and shadow values.

- **Hard Light.** Hard Light is like Soft Light but with more contrast.

- **Color Dodge.** Colorizes the base pixel using the blend pixel hue; light pixels are colorized more than dark pixels.

- **Color Burn.** Colorizes the base pixel using the blend pixel hue; dark pixels are colorized more than light pixels.

- **Darken.** Applies the darker of the base and blend colors, but only where the base color is lighter than the blend color. Where the base color is darker, pixels aren't changed.

- **Lighten.** Applies the lighter of the base and blend colors, but only where the base color is darker than the blend color. Where the base color is lighter, pixels aren't changed.

- **Difference.** Applies the color value that results from subtracting one color from another. Bigger differences between base and blend pixel colors increases the effect, but identical pixels result in black.

- **Exclusion.** A lower-contrast version of the Difference mode.

- **Hue.** Applies the base color's lightness and saturation and the blend color's hue.

- **Saturation.** Applies the base color's lightness and color and the blend color's saturation.

- **Color.** Applies the base color's lightness and the blend color's hue and saturation.

- **Luminosity.** Applies the base color's hue and saturation and the blend color's luminance. This mode creates the opposite of the Color blending mode.

Blend Options

If you select Show Options from the Transparency palette's flyout menu, you get two more checkboxes to play with.

- **Isolate Blending.** This limits the effect of grouped objects' individual blending modes to other objects within the group, without affecting objects behind the group.

- **Knockout Group.** This limits the effect of grouped objects' individual blending modes to objects outside the group.

Color & Transparency

Blend Space

When you blend objects using the Transparency command they are converted either to CMYK or RGB for display purposes—you can determine which color mode by selecting one from the Transparency Blend Space submenu (under the Edit menu). If you create documents for print, select the CMYK option. If you create InDesign documents for viewing online, select the RGB option.

Applying Drop Shadows

You can apply a drop shadow to anything on your InDesign page: imported graphics, text frames, lines, and even tables. Drop shadows are an effect attached to an object, so they can be edited or removed at any time. Apply a drop shadow by choosing a frame with the Selection tool and selecting Drop Shadow from either the Object menu or the context menu (or press Command-Option-M/Ctrl-Alt-M)—then turn on the Drop Shadow checkbox. If you select a text frame with a fill color of None, InDesign applies the drop shadow to the text; if the fill is any other color, the drop shadow applies to the frame itself.

The Drop Shadow dialog box lets you set the shadow's color, opacity, and blending mode. You can also determine the location of the shadow—by entering an X and Y offset—and the size of the shadow (how diffuse it is) using the Blur value.

Applying Feathering

The Feather feature (in the Object menu or the context menu) lets you create a soft edge to any object—even text or imported graphics. In the Feather dialog box you can specify the Feather Width and corner appearance (sharp, rounded or diffused). If the command has no effect or makes the original object disappear, the Feather Width value is probably too low or too high.

PART 10

Long Documents

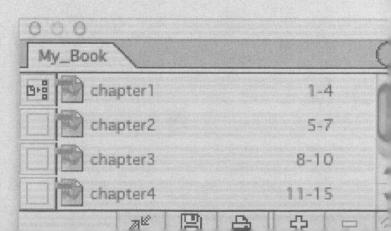

Managing Book Files

InDesign's Book feature lets you effectively manage a number of related files, maintain consistent styles and color definitions across them, and even print them all at once. This is similar to the book features in both Page-Maker and QuarkXPress, but InDesign offers several additional features. For example, you can preflight, package, and export multiple documents from a book to PDF in one easy step.

Building a Book

If you're familiar with how to build books in XPress, you'll feel right at home here. You create books by choosing Book from the New submenu (under the File menu). This opens a Book palette, into which you can then add individual InDesign files by using the Add Document command from the flyout menu or clicking the plus icon at the bottom of the palette. You can also drag InDesign files from the Finder (Macintosh) or Explorer (Windows) into the palette.

The Book palette (and the accompanying book file on disk) just stores references to the InDesign files that you add; the documents aren't embedded into the book file. Because of this you will always need to keep both the book file and the original InDesign documents. While they do not need to be stored in the same folder, they need to be accessible to each other—such as on the same network or on the same computer.

Standardizing Attributes

One reason to use the Books feature is to standardize paragraph styles, character styles, swatches, table of contents styles, and trap styles across multiple documents. You can do this by identifying one document as the source document that will be used as the standard for all other documents in the book. By default the source document is the first file you added to the book, but you can change this by clicking to the left of the name of any document in the palette.

Then you can synchronize the entire book by choosing the Synchronize Book command from the flyout menu (see Figure 40-1) or—just like XPress—by clicking the Synchronize icon at the bottom of the Book palette. If you first select two or more documents in the palette, InDesign will only synchronize those files.

If a style or swatch exists in the source document but not in another book document, it will be added to the book document. If the styles or swatches conflict, those used in the source document will be used to replace the conflicting styles. You can also select which attributes InDesign will synchronize (and which it won't) by selecting Synchronize Options from the flyout menu prior to synchronizing the pages (see Figure 40-2).

Setting Page Order

Another good reason to use the Book feature is to standardize automatic page numbering across multiple documents. InDesign can use the order

Figure 40-1
Although you create and open a book from the File menu, it opens as a separate palette.

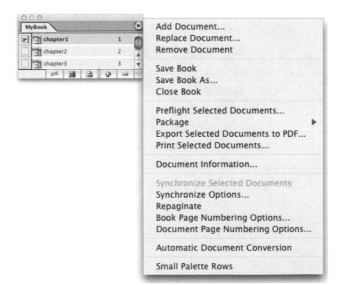

Figure 40-2
Using the
Synchronize
Options dialog
box, you can select
which attributes are
standardized across
book chapters.

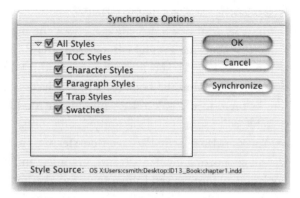

of the files in the Book palette to correctly set the starting page number for each document in the book. You can set the page order of your documents by dragging them up or down within the Book palette. After you drag a document, InDesign renumbers all the other files (which can take a little while).

InDesign (unlike XPress) lets you specify how InDesign should number the pages in your book by selecting Book Page Numbering Options from the Book palette's flyout menu (see Figure 40-3). For example, you can force each chapter to start on either odd or even pages, and you can even tell InDesign to insert blank filler pages when needed. You can also indicate if page numbering should be continued from one chapter to the next. Of course, this only works when you've used automatic page numbering to display your page numbers (see Chapter 18).

Figure 40-3
With the Book
Page Numbering
Options dialog box,
you can set how each
document in a book
will be numbered.

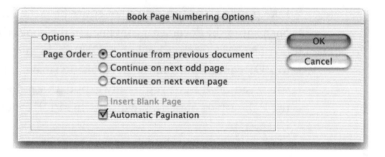

Preparing, Printing, and Exporting Books

A great time saving feature of books is the ability to preflight, package, print, or export multiple documents without manually opening each one.

Preparing Books for Printing

Before you print or export, you can check the preparedness of all files in a book by choosing Preflight Book from the Book palette's flyout menu (XPress and PageMaker don't have this feature). InDesign checks all the documents listed in the book (or all the selected files, if you have chosen one or more in the palette) for missing or modified images along with possible color space problems and missing fonts.

You can also use the Package Book feature (in the flyout menu) to collect all supporting elements (fonts, graphics, and so on) used within the book's documents to send them to a coworker or output provider. This is similar to XPress's Collect for Output feature, but XPress can't "package" up all of the files in a book. We discuss InDesign's Package and Preflight features in detail in Chapter 42.

Printing Books

You can print an entire book—even if it includes many files—without the need to open a single document by clicking the printer icon at the bottom of the Book palette or selecting Print Book from the book palette's flyout menu. As with synchronizing, preflighting, and packaging you can select a portion of the book to print as opposed to the entire book (Command/Ctrl click to select non-contiguous files in the palette). Note that while XPress cannot currently write book files to disk as PostScript, InDesign has no trouble with this. We talk about printing in Chapter 43.

Exporting Books to PDF

Like printing, you can export an entire book to PDF without having to open any of the documents contained in the book (XPress and PageMaker do not allow exporting books to PDF). To do this, select the Export Book to PDF command from the flyout menu (make sure no files are selected when you do this, or you'll only export those documents), and choose the PDF export options. We discuss the PDF export options available in Chapter 44.

41

Table of Contents and Index

As long as you have used paragraph styles throughout your document, InDesign can automatically create a table of contents (TOC) from your document—or even a group of documents, if you are using the Book feature. InDesign can also build an index for your document, though it cannot make it automatically; you have to index entries manually. Here's how it works.

Building a TOC

The TOC feature works almost exactly like the Lists feature in Quark-XPress and the Create TOC feature in PageMaker, though the interface is a bit different. InDesign makes a table of contents in one step, using the Table of Contents feature (which you can select from the Layout menu; see Figure 41-1).

In the Table of Contents dialog box you can enter a title (like "Contents"). Next, identify the paragraph styles to be used in building the table of contents. To do this, double-click each style you want to include in the Other Styles section of the Table of Contents dialog box (or click once and press the Add button). This adds the styles to the Include Paragraph Styles list. You can tell InDesign what paragraph styles to apply to the text within the table of contents you are building by selecting each style from the Include Paragraph Styles list and then choosing a paragraph style from the Entry Style pop-up menu.

Figure 41-1
The Table of
Contents dialog
box lets you identify
which paragraph
styles InDesign
should include in
your TOC and how
they are formatted.

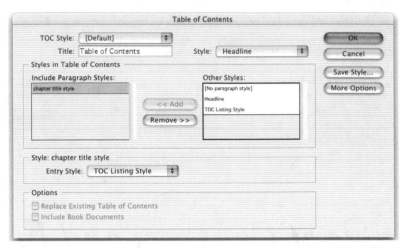

If you are updating an existing table of contents, select the Replace Existing Table of Contents option, and if you are building a table of contents from several Book files, select the Include Book Document option.

When you're ready, click OK. InDesign builds the table of contents and changes the cursor to the Place icon. You can fill an already-made text frame, or just click on the appropriate page to have InDesign create a frame and fill it with the table of contents.

TOC Styles

Just because the feature is called Table of Contents doesn't mean you have to only use it to create tables of contents. Just like XPress's Lists feature, you can make a list of advertisers, a list of illustrators, and a table of contributing authors, all in the same document. The trick is having InDesign keep track of various groups of paragraph styles. These groups of styles are saved as *table of contents styles*, each of which specify a different set of paragraph styles that InDesign is watching, and the paragraph styles that are used to format the text of the list or TOC. You can save all of the settings from the Table of Contents dialog box to easily access them again by clicking the Save Style button. Later, to call up the settings for each style, choose the style name from the TOC Style pop-up menu in the Table of Contents dialog box.

Building an Index

Both QuarkXPress and PageMaker have more or less the same functionality when it comes to building an index, but neither of them lets you make one automatically—and neither does InDesign. Indexing manually is tough and often tedious, though these tools can speed the process for you a little. Because few people need indexing, we only offer the basics here. For an in-depth look, see *Real World InDesign CS*.

Indexing Topics

Some folks start indexing with a list of topics (or entries) they want to use in an index. For example, if you are writing about animals, you might want to predefine topics (categories) for Felines and Canines, even before starting the indexing process. To create a list of topics, open the Index palette from the Window menu and click the Topic button located along the top of the palette (see Figure 41-2). Then select the New Topic command from the palette menu or click the New icon at the bottom of the palette. Later, you can attach specific entries, called references, in your document to the topics you have added. Creating a list of topics is optional.

Making References

Whether or not you have pre-defined index topics, you can start indexing by clicking the Reference button at the top of the Index palette, selecting a word or phrase in your document that you would like to be indexed, and choosing the New Page Reference command from the palette menu or clicking the New icon at the bottom of the palette. This opens the Page Reference Options dialog box, which lets you specify a type (should the entry list this page only or should it list a range of pages) and create nested

Figure 41-2

The Topic option in the Index palette lets you predefine index topics prior to adding references.

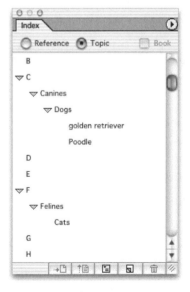

entries so that the selected reference appears beneath a specific topic (see Figure 41-3).

You can indicate that the index should reference the specific location where your cursor was located when you added the reference, that the topic is located on a range of pages, or even that it should be a cross-reference (such as "*See also* Bovine"). You can determine this from the Type pop-up menu when in the Page Reference Options dialog box.

To change an index entry or page reference, you can double-click on the entry in the Index palette.

Building the Index

Once you have added all the page references, you can tell InDesign to go and get the page numbers and build the index by selecting Generate Index from the Index palette menu. InDesign changes the cursor to the Place icon, and you can click on any text frame to place the index. You can also click where no frame exists to have InDesign build a frame for you.

Figure 41-3
Making a new page reference.

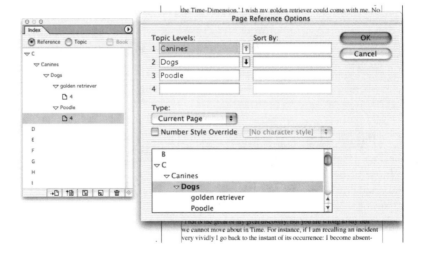

PART 11

Printing

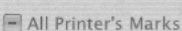

Print

Printer Style: Custom

Printer: PostScript® File

PPD: AGFA SelectSet 5000-X

General
Setup
Marks &Bleeds
Output
Graphics
Color Management

Marks & Bleeds

Marks

☐ All Printer's Marks
  ☑ Crop Marks
  ☐ Bleed Marks

42

Preparing for Print

InDesign provides two fantastic options that help get your documents ready for printing: preflighting and packaging. Preflighting is an inspection of your document and linked elements, including fonts and graphics, so you can see if anything is missing or incorrectly prepared for printing. Packaging is what QuarkXPress calls "Collect for Output"—it grabs everything you need to send your file off to print, from fonts to linked graphics.

Preflighting Your Document

Neither QuarkXPress nor PageMaker offer a comprehensive preflight option, so unless you have experience with a dedicated Preflight software package, this feature may be new for you. Fortunately, it is very straightforward. You can preflight an InDesign document at any time.

The Preflight Dialog Box

Whenever you want to use this feature, choose Preflight from the File menu (or press Command-Option-Shift-F/Ctrl-Alt-Shift-F). In all but the smallest and simplest documents, you'll see a progress bar as InDesign analyzes the document and prepares a report which is presented in the Preflight dialog box. In the Summary panel (see Figure 42-1), areas of concern are highlighted with a triangle warning icon.

To get more information on any of the areas that were inspected in the preflight, click on the panels in the left column.

Printing

Figure 42-1

The Summary panel
of the Preflight
dialog box

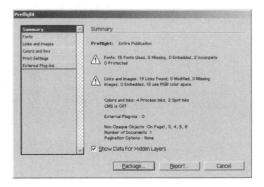

- **Fonts panel.** The Fonts panel lists all the fonts in your document including those used in any linked EPS and PDF files (see Figure 42-2). If you use many fonts, you may want to turn on the Show Problems Only option.

- **Links and Images panel.** The Links and Images panel lists the document's embedded and linked files. For each image, InDesign lists the file format and color space, but unfortunately, the program can't detect RGB color information embedded in EPS or PDF files.

- **Colors and Inks.** The Colors and Inks panel shows you the inks used in your document, including inks specified in EPS or PDF files. This can be useful to identify a document where you have more spot colors than you expect.

- **Other panels.** The Print Settings panel summarizes the current settings in the Print dialog box. The External Plug-ins panel identifies any plug-ins which are required to reproduce the document.

The Cancel button closes the dialog box—however, if you have resolved font or link problems within the Preflight dialog box, those changes are not undone. Click the Report button if you want to save a text file listing the information from the dialog box. Click Package to collect the document and its associated files, which we talk about later in this chapter.

Separation Preview

Another helpful option in checking your documents before printing them is the Separation Preview feature. You can use this to confirm that black text is really black or that a spot color logo is printing using the correct ink. To access this palette, choose it from the Output Preview submenu (under the Window menu).

In the Separations Preview palette, select Separations from the View drop-down menu (see Figure 42-3). InDesign displays all the colors used

Figure 42-2
The Fonts panel
of the Preflight
dialog box

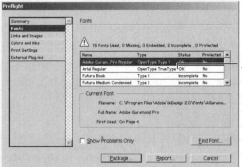

No fonts are missing from this document, but two are incomplete—they are PostScript Type 1 fonts which are missing either their screen or printer font.

Figure 42-3
Separations Preview

in the document and you can turn on and off the visibility of each color plate in the left column (the one with the eyeballs).

Note that InDesign can also display Ink Limit violations and transparency flattener alerts. David covers both of these advanced features in more detail in *Real World InDesign*.

Packaging a Document for Print

After you've confirmed that your document has all of the elements needed for print and you've checked the separations, packaging is the next stage of preparing a document for print. Packaging is the equivalent of QuarkXPress's Collect for Output feature or PageMaker's Prepare for Service Provider feature—it assembles a copy of the publication along with a copy of associated graphics and a copy of fonts used in the document. It also creates a report about the document, which you can give to a service provider or anyone else who might need a copy of your document.

You can package a document in one of two ways. If you have already performed a preflight, just click the Package button in the Preflight dialog box. Or, you can choose Package from the File menu (or press Command-Option-Shift-P/Ctrl-Alt-Shift-P). When you choose Package from the File Menu (or use the key commands) InDesign automatically preflights the document before packaging.

Printing

Before InDesign packages the files, it displays the Printing Instructions dialog box, into which you can enter contact information and any special printing instructions. This information gets added to the automatically-generated report, which also includes information about your document (graphics and fonts used, and so on). After entering the printing instructions, click Continue.

Packaging Options

Next, InDesign lets you choose how your document is packaged. In Windows, this is called the Package Publication dialog box, while on the Macintosh, it's the Create Package Folder dialog box (see Figure 42-4). Here you specify a name and location for the folder which will contain the files.

The document and the Printing Instructions report are always copied into the folder. However, you can choose which other items to include. You'll almost always want to use the default choices: copying the fonts, copying linked graphics, and updating the graphic links in the package. Choosing to update graphic links ensures that when your recipient opens the file, all the graphics will be linked and up-to-date. If your file has layers that are turned off (made invisible), turning on the Include Fonts and Links from Hidden Layers option ensures that required components from those layers are also copied. Turning on the Use Document Hyphenation Exceptions checkbox tells InDesign to embed your customized user dictionary in the document, ensuring that there will be no last minute text reflow problems.

When you're finished choosing options, click Package. If you are copying fonts, an alert from the Adobe Legal Department appears warning of the dangers of sending fonts to people who don't own them (as much as we respect the message, we sure wish we could disable this). Click OK to complete the packaging process.

Figure 42-4
Package Publication
dialog box (called
Create Package
Folder on the
Macintosh)

43

Printing

It is difficult for us to discuss the Print dialog box because of the differences in how printing is handled in each operating system. Adobe has made an admirable effort to make InDesign's Print dialog box look as similar as possible in both Macintosh and Windows (see Figure 43-1). Aside from some minor rearrangements of features within panels, only the buttons at the bottom of the dialog box vary between operating systems: The Macintosh sports Page Setup and Printer buttons; Windows only has a Setup button.

Choosing a Printer

The Printer popup menu in InDesign's Print dialog box displays the printers which you've set up using your operating system and it also displays the option of printing to a PostScript File.

Like QuarkXPress and PageMaker before it, InDesign is designed for PostScript printers. While InDesign also supports non-Postscript printers (like low-cost inkjet printers), many of the Print dialog box choices won't be available. For best results, you may find that exporting a PDF and printing from Acrobat or Acrobat Reader is preferable if you need to print to a non-PostScript printer.

When you pick a PostScript printer, InDesign asks the printer driver for the appropriate PostScript Printer Description (PPD) based upon how the printer was originally set up within the operating system. Although InDesign displays the PPD that is used for each printer, the name is dimmed out unless you are creating a PostScript file.

Figure 43-1
The Print
dialog box
(in Windows)

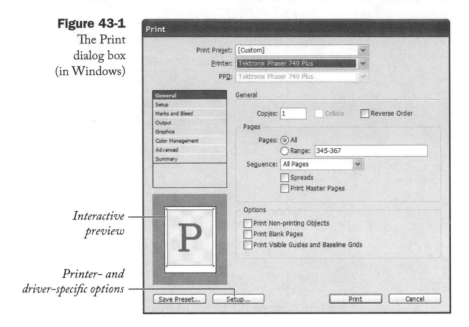

Interactive preview

Printer- and driver-specific options

Creating a PostScript File

We've always thought that writing PostScript to disk is a hassle from QuarkXPress or PageMaker. InDesign lets you export PostScript easily: Just pick PostScript File from the Printer popup menu. You then have the choice to include or exclude printer-specific PostScript code along with the PostScript data created by InDesign. If you know exactly what printer you'll be using when you print the file, then choose its PPD from the PPD popup menu after selecting PostScript file for the printer. Otherwise, choose Device Independent.

Previewing Your Printing

InDesign always provides an interactive preview in the lower-left corner of the Print dialog box. For example, if you change the page size or orientation, or add printer's marks, that will be reflected in the preview. If you click once on the Preview pane, InDesign displays data about your document; if you click again, InDesign shows you how your page will appear on the paper.

Printer-Specific Options

The Print dialog box panels that we describe in this chapter include the features required by almost all printers. However, some printers have special controls which aren't set here (for example, hardware collating features or printer tray selection). You can get access to these options by clicking the Setup button in Windows or the Printer button on the Macintosh.

However, if you see choices in the printer driver (for example, page range) which are also in the InDesign Print dialog box, you should ignore the printer driver setting and make that choice in InDesign.

The General Panel

The Print dialog box's General panel covers the most common printing choices you make. Here you may set any number of copies (up to 999), and even collate them and set the order in which they print.

Just like XPress, you can choose which pages of your document to print, either click All or enter a page range with hyphens (or use commas for discontinuous ranges). To indicate that you want to print an absolute page number, use the plus sign (+) before a page number. This way, you could specify the second page of the document by simply typing +2, even if the page is numbered using roman numerals (such as II).

InDesign offers several other helpful print options here, including whether to print out your master pages, and whether to print nonprinting items (which overrides the Nonprinting object attribute that can be applied to individual objects). You can also choose to print Visible Guides and Baseline Grids—often very helpful during the design process.

The Setup Panel

You can jump to the Setup panel by pressing Command-2/Ctrl-2 (see Figure 43-2). Here you can change paper size and orientation, page scaling and positioning, and you can choose to print thumbnails and tiles.

Paper Size and Orientation

The available paper size choices depend on the selected printer and PPD:

- If you select a printer, the Paper Size popup menu reads Defined by Driver, which means that InDesign uses the current printer driver's default size. You can override this by choosing a different paper size, from the drop-down menu. The choices are based on those specified in that printer's PPD file.

- If you choose to create device independent PostScript, no paper size is available.

- If you choose PostScript targeted for a particular printer, you can also choose the paper sizes listed in that printer's PPD file, or Custom if that is available.

Printing

Figure 43-2

The Print dialog box
Setup panel

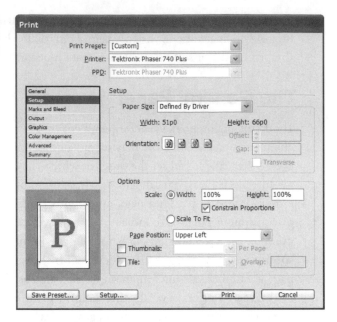

- PPDs for imagesetters and platesetters usually allow the creation of custom paper sizes. When you choose Custom from the Paper Size menu, you may enter any Width or Height value that fits on the paper, but it's much easier to just choose Auto, which automatically calculates the minimum paper size needed to output the current page with all marks and bleeds, reducing media waste to a minimum.

The Orientation feature defines how the page is oriented on the paper (or other media) it's printed on. For high-resolution PostScript imagesetters, which image onto roll-fed material, the PPD may also allow the page to be rotated on the media by choosing the Transverse option.

There are two other options which only appear when selecting roll-fed printers, similar to choices in QuarkXPress: Offset sets the distance between the left edge of the media and the left edge of the page. Gap sets the distance between pages. It's rare that you need to mess with these.

Scaling and Positioning Options

InDesign's Scale Width and Height option allows you to set page scaling from 1 to 1000 percent (much larger and smaller than XPress or Page-Maker). Usually, you'll leave the Constrain Proportions option turned on, forcing InDesign to apply the same scaling to the Height and Width. However, non-proportional scaling is also possible, and can be useful for a specialized printing process like flexography. The Scale to Fit feature works exactly like the Fit in Print Area option in XPress.

Similarly, Page Position is equivalent to the same-named feature in QuarkXPress: It's useful when you are printing a small page on large paper. This is disabled when Scale to Fit, Thumbnails or Tiling is turned on.

Thumbnails and Tiling

You can print several scaled-down pages called thumbnails on a single sheet of paper by turning on the Thumbnails option. Where QuarkXPress only gives you one size of thumbnail, InDesign allows you to select between 2 and 49 thumbnails per page. Use the Preview pane to see how they will fit on your paper.

You may also tile documents like you can in XPress and PageMaker—printing a large page in sections on a smaller paper size—by checking the Tile option and choosing from among Auto (automatically calculates the number of sheets to print on based on the Overlap value, which describes how much an edge is repeated between tiles), Auto Justified (calculates using the Overlap value as a minimum), or Manual (prints a single tile: you set the upper left corner by positioning the ruler zero point).

Marks & Bleed

The Marks & Bleed panel lets you specify which printer's marks should appear around the printed page, as well as how big the bleed area should be (see Figure 43-3).

Printer's Marks

InDesign offers much finer control than either PageMaker or QuarkXPress, letting you turn on or off five different types of page marks:

- **Crop Marks:** Thin rules which tell your commercial printer where to trim the page.
- **Bleed Marks:** Thin rules which mark the bleed area (described below). We rarely turn this on.
- **Registration Marks:** Printer's targets which are used for aligning color plates (so they're only relevant for color separations).
- **Color Bars:** Gray and colored squares used for measuring ink density.
- **Page Information:** This includes the file name, page number, date and time, and plate color name (when printing color separations).

You can set the line thickness of your crop and bleed marks, as well as their distance (Offset) between the edge of the page and the page marks; the default is 6 points, though we usually set this higher, to 9 or 12 points.

Printing

Figure 43-3
The Print dialog box
Marks & Bleed panel

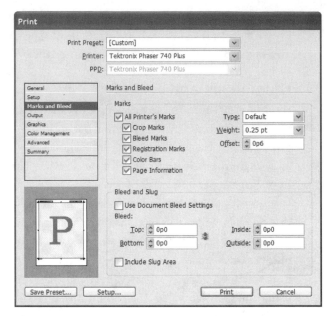

Bleed and Slug Area

When you create artwork that extends all the way to a page edge, you should actually extend it beyond the edge—called a bleed. InDesign only prints objects beyond the page edge if you increase the bleed settings in the Print dialog box. If you specified bleed guides when creating the document, you can simply click "Use Document Bleed Settings"; otherwise, enter the value you need.

Similarly, if you specified a Slug area for your document, you can include that area in your print by turning on the Include Slug Area checkbox.

The Output Panel

Most of the choices you see in the Print dialog box's Output panel are only available when a PostScript printer is chosen (see Figure 43-4). For instance, on a non-PostScript printer—like those ubiquitous Epson ink-jets—only the Color menu and Text as Black option are available.

Kinds of Output

Are you producing a composite color proof, a grayscale print, or do you want each color in the document to be printed on a separate printing plate? The Color popup menu is where you make that choice:

- **Composite Leave Unchanged.** With this option, InDesign sends all the colors to the printer (or PostScript) without converting them.

- **Composite Gray.** Any colors in the InDesign file are converted to grays, though the program can't change colors inside EPS or PDF graphics.

- **Composite RGB.** InDesign sends full-color RGB to the printer. This is best for RGB printers like inkjet printers or film recorders.

- **Composite CMYK.** InDesign sends full-color CMYK to the printer as a single composite file (no separations).

- **Separations.** InDesign sends the data as CMYK separations with each color (including spot colors) on a separate plate. This is best for pre-separated CMYK workflows.

- **In-RIP Separations.** InDesign sends the data as composite CMYK optimized for separation within the printer's (RIP). This choice is only available if you have chosen the PPD of an imagesetter or platesetter which has this capability.

The Text as Black option turns all text to black (as long as it's not colored None, Paper, or a zero-percent tint).

Color Separations

If you choose color separations—either InDesign's or In-RIP—several additional choices become available, such as trapping and flip. We'll cover the Trapping option later in this chapter. The Flip choice allows you to print the page so it images right-reading or wrong-reading and on the correct emulsion side when producing film output. The Negative choice turns

Figure 43-4
The Print dialog box
Output panel

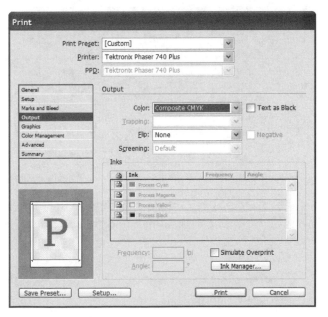

black to white, and *vice versa*, to produce film negatives. While it's nice that InDesign can do these things, output providers often control this stuff and you shouldn't really change these unless you have a specific need.

The Screening options provide combinations of screen frequency (in lines per inch) and output resolution (in dots per inch) for printing.

Choosing and Changing Inks

The Inks list displays all the colors applied in the document. Click the icon to the left of the ink name to tell InDesign whether to print that plate. Each ink listed has a screen frequency and screen angle which is determined by the chosen PPD and the chosen screening/output resolution, as described above.

InDesign's Ink Manager (see Figure 43-5) lets you choose whether each individual spot color prints on its own plate, is converted to a process color. You can even use the Ink Manager to *alias* one spot color to another. For example, perhaps you have used Pantone 471 and Pantone 286, but later need to "merge" them together onto one plate. To alias one to the other, select a color in the Ink Manager and then select the other color from the Ink Alias popup menu.

The other ink characteristics shown here—Type, Neutral Density and Sequence—are related to trapping. Note that the Ink Manager is also available in the Export EPS and Export PDF dialog boxes and in the Swatches palette.

Figure 43-5
The Ink Manager
dialog box

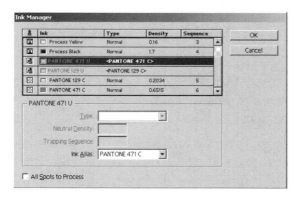

Note that you should only turn on the Simulate Overprint checkbox when printing to proofing printers (like inkjets); it's not for final output.

Trapping

Trapping is the process of compensating for the fact that printing presses sometimes don't align (called *misregistration*), creating unsightly gaps between areas of adjacent colored inks. When a trap is created, objects on the page overlap a tiny amount to prevent the white gaps. While newer presses and processes like direct-to-plate reduce the need for trapping, it is not entirely eliminated.

Many printing professionals turn off the limited trapping options in XPress and PageMaker and use professional trapping software and hardware instead. When you print composite color from InDesign, it will not build in any traps. However, if you are printing color separations, InDesign can apply trapping. InDesign offers two kinds of trapping from the Trapping popup menu in the Output panel: built-in trapping and In-RIP trapping. InDesign's built-in trapping is surprisingly good, and can handle most trapping needs. However, if your output provider has a PostScript 3 RIP which has In-RIP trapping, InDesign can support that (make sure you have the proper PPD chosen for the RIP).

InDesign's trapping engine can correctly handle trapping when objects contain multiple colors, like a gradient, when objects cross multiple colors, and even when objects overlap bitmapped images (TIFF, JPEG and PSD formats). The In-RIP trapping also adds the ability to trap colors within placed EPS, PDF, DCS, and Illustrator graphics.

Because trapping is so specialized based upon the type of print process being used, the printing press (and even the press operator!), we suggest you work closely with your print service provider before using any of these settings. For more details on trapping, see *Real World Adobe InDesign CS*.

The Graphics Panel

The Graphics panel controls how graphics are output, how fonts are sent to the printer, and the kind of data which is sent to the printer (see Figure 43-6). The Images popup menu lets you specify how the data in linked graphics should be sent to the printer:

- **All.** InDesign sends all the high-resolution data from the placed graphic. This is the default, and this should generally be chosen by service providers when sending to a high-resolution printer.

- **Optimized Subsampling.** InDesign samples down the data in bitmap images based on the halftone screen and printer resolution (set in the Output panel). This prints much faster to printers when you're printing low- or medium-resolution proofs.

- **Proxy.** InDesign uses only the low-resolution screen preview data when printing graphics. This is even faster than Optimized Subsampling.

Printing

Figure 43-6

The Print dialog box
Graphics panel

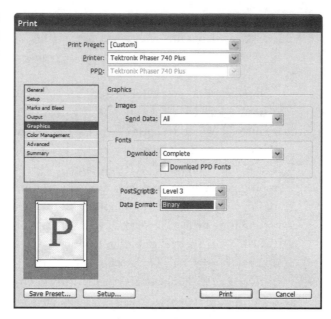

- **None.** InDesign replaces all placed graphics with a large X. This prints the fastest of all, of course.

The Font section controls how fonts get downloaded to the printer. In the Download popup menu, Complete (the default setting) downloads all the document's fonts at the beginning of the print job. Subset downloads only the glyphs (characters) used in the document, but once per page. The None option downloads only references to the fonts and should only be used if you know all the fonts reside on the printer. The Download PPD Fonts checkbox forces all the document's fonts to download, even if the printer's PPD says they are resident in the printer.

Other Panels

InDesign's Print dialog box offers three other panels, too.

- **Color Management.** Color management is such a complex issue that we simply can't cover it sufficiently in this book. We recommend reading *Real World InDesign* or *Real World Color Management* for more details on this topic. Suffice it to say that these features are grayed out unless you enable color management Color Settings.

- **Advanced.** The Advanced Panel is sort of a "catch all." It gives you controls for OPI workflows, for printing gradients to certain kinds of printers, and for choosing transparency flattener settings (see "Printing

Transparency," later in this chapter). For information on anything we've passed-over in this book, look to *Real World Adobe InDesign CS*.

- **Summary.** The Summary panel displays a list of the settings you've made in all the Print dialog panels. We think it's pretty useless, but it may be useful for troubleshooting or communicating with others who are handling your files.

Creating Print Presets

You can save all of the print settings you use for specific printers or certain types of jobs you print. These settings are saved as a *print preset* and they include almost all the choices you can make in InDesign's Print dialog box. If you previously used QuarkXPress, you might have used the Print Styles feature, which is similar to Print Presets.

Creating a Print Preset

The easiest way to create a Print Preset is to open the Print dialog for a typical job in your workflow, set up each of the panels, and then click the Save Preset button at the bottom of the dialog box. That's all there is to it! If you are simply setting up a preset and not printing, you can press Cancel to leave the Print dialog box.

However, if you print to many different devices or you need to edit a number of existing presets, you may find it more efficient to choose Define from the Print Presets submenu (under the File menu). This displays the Define Print Presets dialog box (see Figure 43-7), which list the Default preset (the settings that appear by default in the Print dialog box) as well as any other printer presets you've created. You can then create new Print Presets and you can also edit or delete existing Print Presets.

If you want to save your print presets to share with your colleagues or place them on another computer where you use InDesign, select the presets

Figure 43-7
The Define Print
Presets dialog box

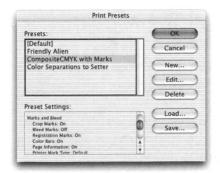

225

to be shared and then click the Save button. Later, you can click the Load button to load the presets into the other computer.

By the way, there are a couple of items in the Print dialog box which cannot be saved in a preset and which must be set individually for a specific job. For instance, specific inks and ink aliasing cannot be saved in a preset as these are job specific options.

Selecting Print Presets

When printing, selecting a print preset is as simple as choosing it from the Print Preset popup menu at the top of the Print dialog box. You can also choose a preset from the Print Preset submenu (under the File menu). If you want to print your entire document with one of your print preset, hold down the Shift key while selecting the preset from the Print Preset submenu—this bypasses the Print dialog box entirely!

Printing Transparency

Transparency is the visual interaction of objects which have differing degrees of opacity. As we explored in Chapter 39, InDesign lets you make objects transparent, and you can import transparent graphics from Illustrator, Photoshop and Acrobat. This gives you some design and production capabilities far beyond what you can create in QuarkXPress or PageMaker. However, you must consider some important consequences of using transparency when printing. The foremost of these is flattening.

Transparency Must Be Flattened

When it comes time to print, the beautiful transparent effects that you've created must be sent to a machine which doesn't know what transparency is. PostScript—the language spoken by most laser printers, imagesetters, and platesetters—only understands objects which are completely opaque. So InDesign (or any application which works natively with transparency) must take the transparent objects and break them into lots of different non-transparent pieces; this process is called *flattening*. The result is a single opaque page that comes out of the printer.

You can control the way flattening occurs by choosing a *transparency flattener preset*, which we discuss below.

When Flattening Happens

When you have transparent objects or graphics containing transparency on a page, flattening happens on three different occasions in InDesign:

- When you print, InDesign uses the flattening settings in the Advanced panel of the Print dialog box.

- When you export an EPS file, InDesign uses the flattening settings in the Advanced panel of the Export EPS dialog box.

- When you export a PDF file in the Acrobat 4 format, InDesign uses the flattening settings on the Advanced panel of the Export PDF dialog box. Acrobat 5 PDF format and later can include transparency so it doesn't have to be flattened.

Figure 43-8 shows four simple objects created in InDesign. To show the effect of flattening, which normally only appears when printed, we exported the file to an Acrobat 4 PDF file. Then we opened the PDF in Adobe Illustrator, where the flattened objects can be observed. To make the effect more apparent, we offset some of the objects so you can see that they were broken into pieces. InDesign doesn't break up the type, but it does convert some of it into a clipping path.

Note that InDesign has to have your high-resolution linked graphics on hand at print time in order to flatten properly, so you can't print through an OPI server.

Figure 43-8
Simple objects with transparency—before and after flattening. Some of the flattened objects were offset to make the results more obvious.

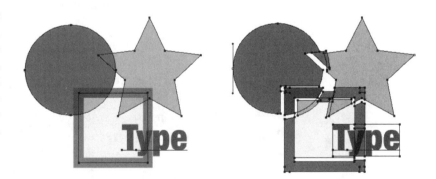

How Can You Identify Transparency?

Don't get caught by surprise when objects get flattened. Anytime you have transparent objects or graphics containing transparency there are three signs you can look for to indicate there is transparency on a spread.

First, a page which has transparency shows a checkerboard background on the Pages palette (see Figure 43-9). Second, when you preflight a document with transparency, the Summary panel lists the pages where there are "non opaque objects."

You can also select Flattener Preview from the Output Preview submenu (under the Window menu). This palette can highlight areas that are

Printing

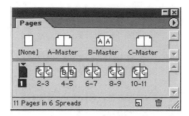

Figure 43-9
A checkerboard background on a page indicates transparency.

impacted by transparency. Choose the types of transparency by selecting from the Highlight drop-down menu in the Flattener Preview palette. Objects that meet the Highlight criteria are highlighted in red while other objects are displayed in grey.

Controlling How Flattening Occurs

Flattening usually adds to the time it takes to print a document—how much extra time depends on the complexity of the page. There's no reason to use the highest quality flattening when printing a proof to a desktop laser printer, so we usually pick Medium Resolution from the Transparency Flattener popup menu in the Advanced panel of the Print dialog box. But you should take the time to get the best quality on an imagesetter or platesetter, so choose High Resolution for final output.

Customizing the Controls

If you're a output service provider, and you really need to fine-tune your transparency output, you can create custom flattener styles by choosing Transparency Flattener Presets from the Edit menu. If you plan to print a great many transparent objects, we suggest you look at *Real World Adobe InDesign* for more details than we're able to provide in this guide.

Resources for Print Service Providers

We expect that some of you reading this book work for output service providers—printers, service bureaus, and the like. We know you'll need more information about printing than we can cover in this book. Fortunately, Adobe provides a number of resources for you: You can find documentation, including known issues, workarounds and tips, at the InDesign Print Service Provider Resources Web site. This page is currently at *http://www. adobe.com/asnprint*. You can also become a member of the Adobe Authorized Service Provider (AASP) program: *http://partners.adobe.com/asn/ programs/printserviceprovider/index.jsp*

PART 12

Exporting

Export PDF

Style: Custom

General
Compression
Marks & Bleeds
Advanced
Security
Summary

Compression

Color Bitmap Images

Bicubic Downsample to

Compression: Automa

Quality: Medium

Exporting EPS and PDF

Sometimes you need to use one or more InDesign pages in another application and you want to save the pages as a graphic. To do this in QuarkXPress or PageMaker, you would save the page as an Encapsulated PostScript file (EPS). InDesign lets you save pages as EPS, but it also lets you save in the more robust PDF format. We cover exporting to these file formats in this chapter.

Export as EPS

Exporting to EPS is quite simple. You can choose Export from the File menu, and then select EPS from the Formats popup menu, give the file a name, and let InDesign do the work. But, like most other things, there are options you can select.

There are two panels of options to control how InDesign saves your EPS file. The General panel provides many of the same selections as on XPress's Save Page as EPS tab (see Figure 44-1). Each EPS file can contain only one page, but InDesign lets you specify a range of pages. For example, if there are ten pages in your document, InDesign creates ten EPS documents, appending the page number to each name. If you have created multipage spread, you can check Spreads, and a single EPS file will be created for each spread.

Format Settings

An EPS file contains both the high-resolution data for the printer and a screen preview. The high-resolution information can be written either for

Figure 44-1

The Export EPS
dialog box
General panel

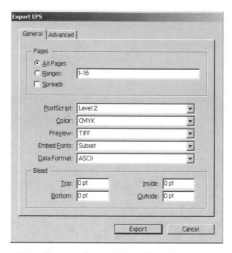

a PostScript Level 2 or Level 3 printer. For Color, there are four choices: CMYK is usually the best choice for print. You can also select RGB (though it's rare you'd need it), Gray to turn color to gray values, or Device Independent if you have enabled color management.

The ability to embed fonts in an EPS file is an improvement from earlier page layout programs. You can set InDesign's Embed Fonts popup menu to Complete (entirely embedded), Subset (to get only the font characters you actually used), or None. For Data Format, you can write the EPS as Binary (more compact and faster) or ASCII (slower, but required by some older networks and printers).

The preview of an EPS file can be TIFF (best for cross-platform use), PICT (only available on a Macintosh), or None.

The Bleed section of the General panel specifies whether the EPS is cut off at the page boundaries or includes objects within a bleed area. You can enter a Bleed amount for each side of the page of up to 6 inches.

Advanced Options

The Advanced panel is used to specify the handling of images, OPI workflows, transparency flattening, and ink manager choices (see Figure 44-2). Generally you'll want to include all the image data rather than use a low-resolution proxy. For those who still use OPI, the workflow choices are the same as are found on the Advanced panel of the Print dialog box.

Transparency always needs to be flattened when saving EPS files, so you also have an option for choosing a transparency flattener style (you should probably use High Resolution). Finally, the Advanced panel also gives you access to the same Ink Manager and overprint simulation features we discussed in the previous chapter.

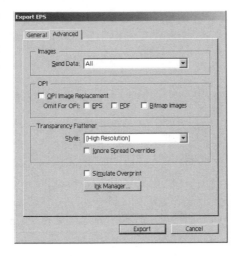

Figure 44-2
The Export EPS
dialog box
Advanced panel

Creating PDF Files

You can export one or more pages to an Adobe PDF file by selecting Export from the File menu and choosing Adobe PDF from the Format popup menu. After you name the file and tell InDesign where to save it, InDesign displays the Export PDF dialog box (see Figure 44-3). The program ships with seven built-in settings for PDF files, listed in the Style popup menu.

- **eBook.** Use this setting for PDF files that will be displayed on screen but may also need to be printed. It is a hybrid between the Screen and Print settings.

- **Screen.** Use this to create the smallest PDF files where a small file size is more important than image quality.

- **Print.** Use this for general office use, when files will be printed on inkjet or laser printers around your office.

- **Press.** Use this to create high quality PDF files that will be sent to your commercial printer for output using various printing methods, including color separations.

- **PDF/X-1a and PDF/X-3.** Use these to create PDF files that conform to the international standard for sharing PDF files, typically used by magazine publishers who receive advertisements in the PDF format.

- **Acrobat 6 Layered.** Use this to preserve your InDesign layers in the Adobe PDF file you are creating. The recipient of the PDF will need Adobe Acrobat 6 to use the layers, however.

Exporting

These built-in settings will likely meet most of your needs. However, you can always override these settings by changing the options in each of the panels of the Export PDF dialog box.

Customizing Your PDF Export

InDesign lets you customize your PDF files in all sorts of ways in the first five of the six panels listed along the left side of the PDF Export dialog box. Note that you can choose these panels by clicking on them; by holding down the Command/Ctrl key while pressing a number, 1 through 6; or by pressing Command/Ctrl-Page Up or Page Down.

While we cover some of the many PDF options here, Christopher's *Real World Adobe Acrobat 6* book has several chapters devoted to settings used when creating PDF files and you can also look to David's *Real World InDesign CS* for more detailed information.

General

Using the options in the General panel (see Figure 44-3), you can specify which pages will be exported, and if adjoining pages should be exported as spreads. Remember that a page range can include commas or hyphens (such as "2, 5-7" to export page 2 followed by pages 5, 6, and 7). The General panel also offers a wide variety of other options. For example, if you created hyperlinks in your file, turn on Include Hyperlinks to make them functional in the PDF. InDesign also lets you specify if PDF bookmarks will be included, but you must have already have used the Table of Contents feature (see Chapter 41) for this to work.

Compression

You can use the Compression panel settings to define the quality of placed bitmapped images in the PDF file. The lower the resolution and the higher the compression, the smaller the file size. But there's a tradeoff: reduced quality. In general, when we're sending a PDF file for final print output, we make sure the Compression popup menus are set to Zip or None—that way we won't get any JPEG compression artifacts.

Note that turning on the Crop Image Data to Frames option helps reduce the size of the file by eliminating data that is not visible. This limits the ability for someone else to later to reposition an image within a frame, but this type of editing is rarely performed in PDF files. The Compress Text and Line Art compresses page objects created in InDesign; we can't think of any reason to ever turn this off.

Figure 44-3
The General panel
of the Export PDF
dialog box

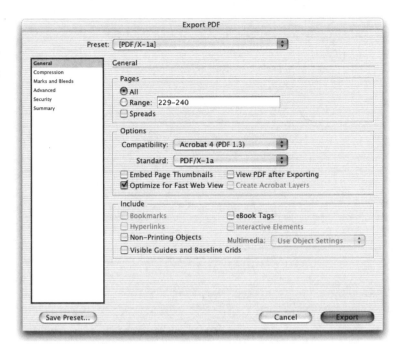

Marks & Bleeds

If you have bled objects off the side of your page, or if you need crop marks around the corners, you'll need to set these up in the Marks & Bleeds panel; the preset Press style doesn't do either of these for you. You can also set the offset (distance from the page) and weight of trim marks you add.

Advanced

You can use the Advanced panel settings to define how color is converted when exporting to PDF (see Figure 44-4). You can choose to have all colors converted to RGB or CMYK , or you can leave them unchanged. If you are setting up all of your colors in Photoshop, Illustrator and InDesign prior to exporting this should probably be set to Leave Unchanged. If you are converting the file for posting to a web site, choose the RGB option.

InDesign also lets you determine whether fonts are embedded completely or subsetted. By setting the Subset Fonts Below setting at a high value (like 100%), InDesign only embeds the characters you use in the PDF file and not the entire font family. If you set this at a lower value (like 0%), the entire font will get embedded and not just the characters used in the document. David likes to set this to zero percent for documents destined for a printer or output provider because he likes the whole font to be embedded, but Christopher and Steve tend to set it to 100 percent. To each their own.

Exporting

Figure 44-4

The Advanced panel of the Export PDF dialog box

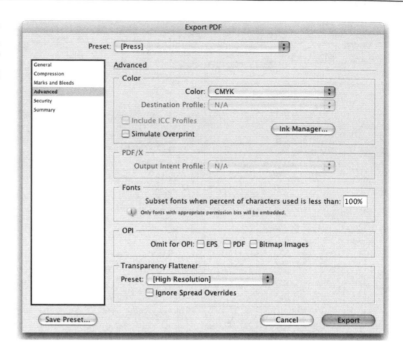

The Advanced panel is also home to the Transparency Flattener popup menu. Make sure you set this to High Resolution before creating a PDF that you'll send for final output.

Security

If you want to make your printer very unhappy, you can apply security to a PDF file to limit access to the file or restrict printing or editing. Use a Master password to restrict someone from changing or removing your security settings; apply an User password if you want users to input a password before viewing the file. Beware that it is very difficult to remove these restrictions if you forget the password. These security settings only apply to the PDF you are creating, not to the original InDesign file.

After you have finished with the Security settings you can then review all of the settings applied to the PDF you're creating by clicking the Summary panel.

PDF Export Presets

You can save the settings you've so carefully chosen in the PDF Export dialog box as a PDF "style" and later call them back up by choosing from the Preset pop-up menu at the top of the dialog box. You can create a PDF preset by choosing PDF Export Presets from the File menu (see Figure 44-5). However, it is much faster to simply set up the PDF Export dialog box the way you like and then click the Save Preset button at the bottom of the dialog box.

After saving a preset, you can recall it in the Export PDF dialog box. However, it's even faster to hold down the Shift key while selecting your preset from the PDF Export Presets submenu (under the File menu). That way you bypass the Export PDF dialog box entirely.

An Alternative to Exporting

Note that you can still use Acrobat Distiller to create PDF files from InDesign. The two-step approach of printing a PostScript file to disk and then having the print-to-disk file processed by Distiller is more time consuming, but sometimes worthwhile. When creating very small PDF files is our highest priority we use Acrobat Distiller—just as we would from QuarkXPress or PageMaker—because InDesign's Export feature almost always makes larger PDF files than a comparable quality PDF file created through Distiller. Also, some PDF files exported PDF files won't print on some printers (primarily older, non-Adobe PostScript emulators, or "clones"). In these cases, we also use the Distiller to create the PDF files.

Figure 44-5
Creating a PDF export preset for your frequently used PDF settings saves time and reduces the possibility of errors.

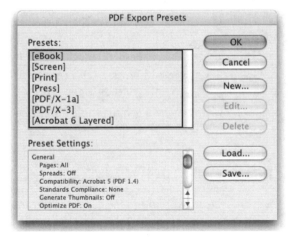

45

Other Export Options

Your InDesign documents are probably designed for printing, but you can also export them for viewing on the Web by exporting your pages as JPEG files, as SVG files, or as files suitable for editing with Adobe GoLive. Here's a quick rundown of several other export options InDesign offers.

Export as JPEG

Feel like turning your one of your document pages into a picture? You can select Export from the File menu, then choose JPEG from the Format popup menu. InDesign lets you pick any page (only one page at a time, though), along with some basic image quality settings (the lower the quality, the smaller the resulting file). Unfortunately, the JPEG is always 72 dpi, so it's appropriate for a Web page and little else. If you need a higher-resolution image, try scaling your whole page up with the Scale tool before exporting the JPEG.

Packaging for GoLive

While both QuarkXPress and PageMaker offer tools for exporting HTML, InDesign's integration with GoLive, a dedicated web site management tool is very helpful. You can then use all of the elements in a web site that is built and maintained in GoLive. Because the needs of a print layout and web layout are very different, we find this approach to be very intelligent.

To export your document for use with GoLive, choose Package for GoLive command from the File menu and tell InDesign where the package files should be saved. You can then choose from two tabs that help refine the way the web package is created.

- **General.** In this panel you can control whether the package is opened in GoLive once it is complete. Make sure that the encoding matches your GoLive web site.

- **Images.** You can control whether the original imported images should be copied into the package or if the images should be optimized into GIFs or JPEGs before being copied. GoLive can use graphics that were imported into InDesign, but graphics created using InDesign's drawing tools can not be brought into GoLive.

Export as XML

By choosing XML from the Format popup menu in the Export dialog box (in Windows, this popdown menu is called Save as Type), you can specify where the XML file will be saved and how image references will be handled. The interface is identical to packaging files for GoLive, as the GoLive package option actually uses XML.

Export as SVG

The Scalable Vector Graphics (SVG) file format is a way to describe vector page objects (text, graphics, shapes, and so on) using XML. Some folks are beginning to post SVG files on the Web as an alternative to the Flash format. But despite acceptance from the W3C and software developers, like Adobe, its use is not widespread. If you are sure that your audience has the SVG plug-in or a standalone viewer that can display SVG files (perhaps your company's sales force, for instance), then you can use InDesign's ability to export to SVG.

Neither PageMaker nor QuarkXPress can export SVG files, though Quark has said they are committed to the format. Figure 45-1 shows the various options you can set in the Export SVG dialog box. Many of these are similar to those in the HTML and PDF export dialog boxes. For more information on exporting to SVG, see *Real World InDesign*.

InDesign Interchange Format

The InDesign Interchange Format (.inx file) is a way to save an entire InDesign file in a text-only file. This feature was intended as a way to save InDesign CS files for use in InDesign 2. You can export your files just

Exporting

Figure 45-1

Export as
SVG options

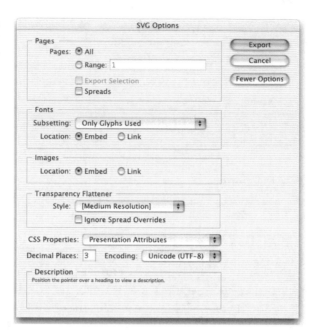

fine, but unfortunately there's no way to open these files in InDesign 2! Therefore .inx files aren't particularly helpful yet. On the other hand, we have found that we can clean up the occasional file "weirdness" (possible document corruption) by exporting the file in the interchange format and then reopening this .inx file in InDesign.

Technically, the InDesign Interchange Format file is saved as an XML file, so technically you could do some interesting things with it if you understood both XML and the file format (which is, sadly, undocumented by Adobe). But in the meantime, we ignore it most of the time.

Converting Files
and Plug-ins

Converting QuarkXPress Files

Perhaps the greatest concern to QuarkXPress users who want to use Adobe InDesign is the large store of XPress files on our hard drives. Fortunately, you can convert most of your QuarkXPress files and templates into InDesign documents. In this appendix, we'll tell you what you need to know to make this feature work for you.

Note that InDesign CS can open QuarkXPress 3.3 and 4.x documents and templates. It can open QuarkXPress Passport files of the same versions if they have been saved as single-language files. QuarkXPress 5 files must be saved backward to QuarkXPress 4 format. Files from XPress 6 are an even bigger hassle: You have to save them as version 5 files, then open them in version 5 and save them down to version 4. (InDesign can also open Adobe PageMaker 6.5 and 7.0 files as well; we talk about that in Appendix B.)

Although we don't know what Adobe has planned for later versions of InDesign, it would surprise us if they ever update this feature so that it can open files from XPress 5 or later; we think of it as a "limited time opportunity."

Conversion Isn't Perfect

When InDesign opens a QuarkXPress file, it must do a file translation into the InDesign format. This is extremely difficult, partly because Quark hasn't made public their secret and proprietary file format information (Adobe had to decode it themselves). Plus, InDesign performs a great many page layout functions differently than XPress does, and there are some XPress features which don't exist at all in InDesign—like layout spaces and most of the Web features. As with translations between spoken languages, conversions from QuarkXPress aren't flawless. It's our experience that InDesign's conversion can get you about 90 percent of the way there in an "average" document.

All but the most simple XPress documents will likely require some reworking in InDesign. The more design-intensive your pages, the more likely you'll have to do significant cleanup. That said, we also know of cases in which very complex pages converted without any changes whatsoever. On the other hand, we have heard of at least one case of a commercial printer opening a customer's XPress files in InDesign without consulting with the client first (because he wanted to print from InDesign instead)—this is clearly a *really bad* idea.

What Translates Well

InDesign can read all the paragraph and character styles, master pages, and RGB or CMYK colors in the XPress document (colors other than CMYK and RGB may be an issue, which we'll discuss below). The page geometry (where things are on the page) and XPress-created and linked items will almost always be converted correctly, but proof the files closely for small "glitches," like objects that have moved slightly. Text formatting will usually be converted well, but many line endings may break slightly differently because InDesign uses a different composition engine.

Think "Templates"

In our opinion, your best strategy is to think about opening templates rather than files. That is, open template files, or open old XPress documents that you're going to significantly update anyway. Use the conversion process to create new InDesign templates which can be used to produce new projects. Or, if you have files that have elements which are frequently used in many documents, convert those files only as needed. Converting all your legacy QuarkXPress or PageMaker documents into InDesign documents is probably a waste of time.

Even if you only work in InDesign from now on, you'll probably still want to keep a copy of XPress around to open old legacy documents. This is just a harsh reality of publishing—David still keeps an old copy of Page-Maker handy to deal with the documents he created in the late 1980s!

Converting QuarkXPress Files

Converting a QuarkXPress file is usually as simple as choosing Open from the File menu, and selecting the file (or dragging the file on top of the InDesign application icon). However, there are a few preliminaries that we recommend you follow which usually make the process go smoother.

First Steps

First, it's a good idea to open your QuarkXPress document in XPress and make sure that all the fonts and graphics are up-to-date. Then, resave and rename the file using Save As. These steps generally eliminate InDesign errors which occasionally pop up, such as, "There was an error reading the file," "The document includes one or more broken links to external image files," and even "Cannot convert the document."

The conversion also generally works the best if linked graphics reside on your local hard drive, rather than on a network server or removable disk. Also, objects created by some third-party XPress XTensions may not convert properly (or at all). If you have trouble converting the file, you may have to disable the problem XTension and resave the file from XPress.

The Conversion Process

When converting a file, InDesign displays a series of messages describing what it's doing. When it finishes, it may display a Conversion Warnings dialog box (see Figure A-1), which lists objects it had trouble converting and missing resources. However, this isn't necessarily a complete list of everything which didn't convert!

Note that opening an XPress file in InDesign takes much longer than simply opening a normal file. The length of time depends entirely on the document's contents, but it's not uncommon for the conversion process

Figure A-1
The Conversion
Warnings dialog box

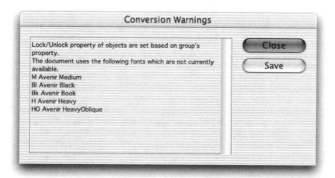

Conversion Warnings

Lock/Unlock property of objects are set based on group's property.
The document uses the following fonts which are not currently available.
M Avenir Medium
Bl Avenir Black
Bk Avenir Book
H Avenir Heavy
HO Avenir HeavyOblique

Close
Save

Appendix

to take several minutes *per page*. This may be a good time to take a break and go get a latté.

Problem Areas to Look For

Always proof your newly converted document carefully. The following list describes some of the areas which are likely to be the most problematic when converting QuarkXPress files, but it's by no means complete.

- **Runaround.** Text wrapping is handled completely differently by each application. It's likely that you'll have to re-apply text wrap to many graphics (see Chapter 33).

- **Clipping Paths.** Images that contain clipping paths usually appear correctly in InDesign, but we've found that inexplicably the clipping paths sometimes get messed up in one way or another. Turning the path off and back on again in the Clipping Paths dialog box usually fixes this (see Chapter 31).

- **Colors.** RGB, CMYK, and Multi-ink colors should translate just fine. However, if you've defined objects using the Pantone, Trumatch, or Focoltone color libraries, these inks will be converted to CMYK definitions. However, they will still be listed as spot colors and separate on their own spot color plates, so this usually isn't a big problem.

- **Keyboard Shortcuts for Styles.** InDesign uses a smaller number of keyboard shortcuts for character and paragraph styles than QuarkXPress. Those shortcuts which don't fit InDesign's restricted range are dropped (the styles are still there, however).

- **Colorized Images.** InDesign supports colorizing only black-and-white and grayscale TIFFs. XPress supports colorizing a few other file formats; these lose their coloring.

- **Nonprinting Images.** Occasionally, some images in a document will become non-printing for no particular reason. You can quickly test to see if this is happening to you by switching into the Preview mode, which hides all non-printing items (see Chapter 4). The fix is simple: Select the image with the Direct Select tool and turn off the Non-printing checkbox in the Attributes palette.

- **Special Characters and Type Styles.** QuarkXPress has a few special characters which don't exist in InDesign. These include the flex space (which is converted to an en space) and the superior style (usually converted to superscript). Bold and italic formatting is only maintained if the true font exists (faux bold or italic will appear on the InDesign page highlighted in pink). Shadow and outline styles aren't supported in InDesign.

Getting Help

Adobe has two Support Knowledgebase documents which are helpful for dealing with conversion issues beyond what we can cover in this book. Support Knowledgebase Document *321f6* lists features which are supported in InDesign and which are not. Document *20b2a* gives some troubleshooting procedures you can follow if conversion fails. Both are available on the Adobe website by searching for these numbers at: *www.adobe.com/search/*

Other Conversion Options

Opening an XPress document in InDesign isn't the only way to transfer your assets to your new page-layout program. You may find that it is easier, faster, or more convenient to transfer just parts of the document and rebuild the file in InDesign from scratch. Here are a few things to keep in mind.

You can export your text stories as Microsoft Word files (or Rich Text Format files in XPress for Windows or XPress 6) and import them into InDesign.

We also find it helpful to use XPress's Collect for Output feature to pull together all the graphics in one place, making them easier to import into InDesign.

One of the best ways to repurpose content from XPress or InDesign or any other program is XML. In our opinion, the Avenue.Quark XML tools that ship with QuarkXPress 6 aren't currently particularly useful. However, there are several other Quark XTensions on the market that help you get XML out of XPress, like RoustaboutXT from Apropos Toy & Tool Development (*www.attd.com*), WebXPress from Gluon (*www. gluon.com*), EasyPress from Atomik (*www.atomik-xt.com*), and Xtract from Noonetime (*www.noonetime.com*). Once you have XML files in hand, you can import them into InDesign. (For more on dealing with XML files in InDesign, see *Real World InDesign.*)

B

Converting PageMaker Files

PageMaker users who are making the transition to InDesign are understandably concerned about how well their PageMaker documents are going to convert in InDesign documents. The good news is that the conversion from PageMaker to InDesign is relatively easy. In this appendix, we'll cover what you can do to prepare for conversion, and what to expect afterwards.

InDesign CS can open documents and templates saved either as PageMaker 6.5 or 7.0 document from either Macintosh or Windows. If you've purchased Adobe's PageMaker Plug-in Pack (see Chapter 2), you should also be able to open PageMaker 6.0 files.

Preparing for Conversion

It's always best to work on a copy of a PageMaker document when doing a conversion. If the file exists on a network server, floppy disk or other removable media, copy the PageMaker document and all its linked graphics onto your local hard drive for best results.

Updating Fonts and Graphics
The first step in converting a PageMaker document is to open it in Adobe PageMaker, and update the fonts and graphics. When you open the file, the program should warn you of any missing fonts. If possible, find and open the correct fonts. If necessary use the Substituted Font popup menu, to select replacement fonts.

You should also receive warnings of graphics which are missing. Link to any missing graphics while you're opening. If you can't relink, after you open the document, go to the Links Manager dialog box, and relink the graphics there. If you can't find the original on disk, it's probably better just to delete the picture from the file.

InDesign works best when all graphics are linked and not embedded. Fortunately, PageMaker has a utility which allows you to globally unembed and relink your graphics. To use this utility, select Utility > Plug-ins > Global Link Options. You can select "Change options for graphics," and *deselect* "Store copy in pub." At the top of the dialog box, select All pages of the document. When you click OK, you may have to wait a few minutes while PageMaker processes your request.

Resaving the Document

Both PageMaker and InDesign files tend to get larger as we work with them over time. Before opening a PageMaker file in InDesign, you want to save it as small as possible to remove any unnecessary hidden information. Go to PageMaker preferences, and, if necessary, select the Save Smaller option. Then choose File > Save As to resave your document.

Opening the File in InDesign

Opening a PageMaker document or template is as simple as choosing Open from the File menu and selecting the file. In Windows, choose PageMaker (6.0-7.0) in the Files of Type menu. Select the PageMaker file, and click Open. Or, you can just drag the PageMaker file on top of the InDesign application icon on the desktop.

When converting a file, InDesign displays a series of messages describing its progress. When it finishes, it may display the Conversion Warnings dialog box (see Figure B-1). which lists objects it had difficulty converting

Figure B-1
The Conversion Warnings dialog box

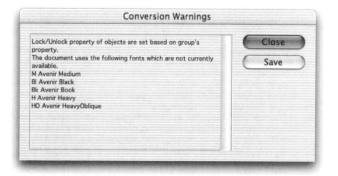

Conversion Warnings

Lock/Unlock property of objects are set based on group's property.
The document uses the following fonts which are not currently available.
M Avenir Medium
Bl Avenir Black
Bk Avenir Book
H Avenir Heavy
HO Avenir HeavyOblique

Close
Save

Appendix

or resources like fonts and graphics which were missing. However, the list is provided probably won't alert you to every problem.

Conversion Issues

While InDesign does a remarkably good job of converting PageMaker documents, you'll notice a number of discrepancies between the original document and the converted file. Some of these are simply because of differences between the way the two applications work. Here are some common issues:

- **Double-sided Pages.** InDesign converts double-sided documents that do not contain facing pages into single-page spreads. If there are facing pages, they'll be converted to facing-page spreads.

- **Pasteboard.** Because of differences in the way the applications handle pasteboards (see Chapter 2), all items on PageMaker pasteboards will appear on the pasteboard of the first InDesign spread.

- **Layers.** When converting a PageMaker publication, InDesign creates two layers—Default and Master Default. Objects on PageMaker master pages appear on the Master Default layer.

- **Type Composition.** PageMaker composes its lines one line at a time. InDesign's default is the Multi-line Composer which will break lines differently. Even if you choose the Single-line Composer, while the lines may break more similarly, text will usually reflow.

- **Type Styling.** PageMaker can stylize a font (for example, bold or italic) when the printer font is not available, but InDesign cannot. If a printer font is missing when the file is converted, the font is highlighted in pink as missing.

- **Paragraph rules.** Paragraph rules in PageMaker are considered as part of the paragraph slug; in InDesign they're not. Rules above and below extend in opposite directions in the two applications, so they'll have to be reformatted in InDesign.

Think Templates

In our opinion, your best strategy is to think about opening templates rather than files. That is, open template files, or open old PageMaker documents that you're going to significantly update anyway. Use the conversion process to create new InDesign templates which can be used to produce new projects. Or, if you have files that have elements which are frequently used in many documents, convert those files only as needed. Converting all your legacy PageMaker documents into InDesign documents is probably a waste of time.

Even if you only work in InDesign from now on, you'll probably still want to keep a copy of PageMaker around to open old legacy documents. This is just a harsh reality of publishing—David still keeps PageMaker around to deal with the documents he created in the late 1980s!

Getting Help

Adobe has a Knowledgebase article (number *1de22*) which describes what happens to various PageMaker features, settings, and elements when you open PageMaker publications in InDesign. This is available on the Adobe website by searching at *www.adobe.com/search/*

InDesign Plug-ins

When deciding to switch to InDesign, you might have wondered if your existing QuarkXPress XTensions or PageMaker plug-ins would work with InDesign. The answer is no, because XTensions and plug-ins are always customized for a particular software program. Similarly, macros and scripts that work in XPress or PageMaker will not work in InDesign.

What Are Plug-ins?

InDesign may not be able to do everything you'd want, such as the ability to easily create mathematical equations for textbook publishing, arrange pages in printers spreads for offset printing, or interact with databases. Fortunately, you can buy third-party plug-ins that add these additional capabilities.

Most people don't realize that, unlike XPress, most of the features in InDesign are actually plug-ins written by Adobe, and that the application itself is sort of a glorified plug-in manager! This underlying technology has some advantages, like the ability for Adobe to update individual features easily.

Managing Plug-ins

XPress lets you turn on and off XTensions using the XTensions Manager; InDesign can do the same thing with the Configure Plug-ins dialog box (which is available from either the application menu or the File menu, depending upon your operating system). If you never use Navigator palette or the Indexing feature, then you can turn off those plug-ins, making the program launch and run slightly faster.

To enable or disable a plug-in in the Configure Plug-ins dialog box, click in the column to the left of the plug-in name (see Figure C-1). Plug-ins with a lock icon are required by InDesign and may not be disabled. Some plug-ins are required by other plug-ins; if you try to turn one of these off, the program alerts you (and if you still agree to turn it off, the other plug-ins will be disabled, too). After making changes you must quit and restart the program for the new settings to become active.

You can create a new plug-in set by clicking the Duplicate button. Then turn off the plug-ins that you don't need.

Third-Party Plug-ins

Several dozen plug-ins have been created by third-parties. When you want to expand your capabilities with advanced tools, check out the plug-ins from ALAP, Gluon, Em Software, and other developers. There are several distributors of plug-ins, including The Power XChange (which you can find at *www.thepowerxchange.com*) and Plugins World (*www.pluginsworld.com*). You can also find information about plug-ins here: *www.indesignuser-group.com/thirdparty/plug_ins/_plug_ins.php*

Figure C-1
The Configure
Plug-ins dialog box

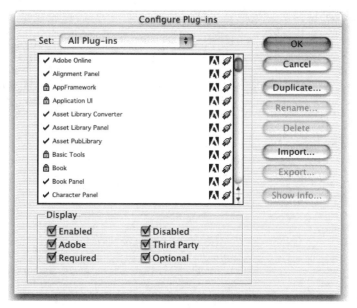

index